CROSVILLE ON MERSEYSIDE

by

T.B. Maund FCIT

Series Editor
Alan Townsin

with additional photography by
Reg Wilson
and
other contributors

TRANSPORT PUBLISHING COMPANY LTD : GLOSSOP : DERBYSHIRE : ENGLAND

ISBN 0 86317 168 0

Other titles by the same author:

Mersey Ferries Vol 1
Transport Publishing Co Ltd 1992

With J. B. Horne
Liverpool Transport Vol 1 1830-1900
Light Railway Transport League 1976
Liverpool Transport Vol 2 1900-30
Light Rail Transit Association & Transport Publishing Co Ltd 1982
Liverpool Transport Vol 3 1931-39
Light Rail Transit Association & Transport Publishing Co Ltd 1987
Liverpool Transport Vol 4 1939-57
Transport Publishing Co Ltd 1989
Liverpool Transport Vol 5 1957-86
Transport Publshing Co Ltd 1991

With M. Jenkins
The Tramways of Birkenhead and Wallasey
Light Rail Transit Association 1987

Typeset and produced for the Publishers by
Mopok Graphics, 128 Pikes Lane, Glossop, Derbyshire
Printed and bound in Great Britain

CONTENTS

Photo Credits

AEC Ltd	31
J.N. Barlow	16, 44 left, 102c&l
Commercial postcard	24u
Crosville Motor Services	6l, 7, 9, 10, 14, 15, 21r, 26, 27u, 33l, 35l, 37, 41l, 44r, 82, 83, 95 both, 96 both, 103
Crosville Archive Trust Collection	6u, 11, 12
D.S. Deacon	21 left
ECW Ltd	42, 99 all
N.N. Forbes	53c, 91l
N.N. Forbes Collection	89l
R.N. Hannay	85u, 90l
J.F. Higham	25
Leyland/TPC Archive courtesy BCVM	24l, 27l, 29l, 36 both, 84l, 97l, 110l
Liverpool City Engineer	29c
R.F. Mack	57l, 85u&c, 104c
R. Marshall	110c
T.B. Maund Collection	22, 29u, 84u, 109l, 111 all
G.D. Parry Collection (courtesy T. Turner)	6l, 23
B.J. Rusk	56c&l, 57u, 59, 60 all, 61 all, 71c, 73, 79l, 93 both, 105
K.W. Swallow	46, 50l, 54, 55, 92 both
TPC Collection	32, 35u, 90c
Tramway & Railway World	39r
T. Turner	47u
T. Turner Collection	20c, 33u, 97u, 110u
Unkown	13, 30, 40, 88u&c, 89u
J.P. Williams	41u, 45, 46, 48, 53l, 87, 88l, 89c, 91u, 98, 101 all, 102u, 104l, 106u
R. L. Wilson	5, 7u&c, 8, 20u, 33c, 39 left, 44u, 47c&l, 49, 50u&c, 51 all, 53u, 56u, 62 all, 64, 65 both, 66, 67 all, 68 all, 70 all, 71 u&l, 74 all, 75 all, 76, 77 all, 78, 79 u&c, 80 both, 85l, 86, 90u, 91c, 104u, 106 c&l, 107, 112 both
Wirral Borough Libraries	18 both

INTRODUCTION

CROSVILLE – 85 YEARS

Origins

In 1906 the Crosville Motor Co. Ltd. was formed with premises at Crane Wharf, Chester for the purpose of manufacturing motor cars and marine engines. The company's name was derived from those of its founders, George Crosland-Taylor and Georges Ville, a Frenchman from whom a number of designs for motor vehicles had been purchased. The Taylor family had been on the fringe of transport for some time, George and his brother James having founded what later became the Helsby Cable Works at Neston in 1882 and James was a director of G.F. Milnes and Co. Ltd., the tramcar manufacturer of Cleveland Street, Birkenhead.

Crosland was Taylor's mother's maiden name and suggests an association with Crosland Moor on the outskirts of Huddersfield where he had been born in 1857. He was always called by this name, not George, and in due course he passed it on to his three sons.

Crosville had little success as a motor manufacturer and in January 1911 started a bus service between Chester and Ellesmere Port. A second route between Kelsall and Chester was purchased from a Mr. Lightfoot, together with a Lacre bus. By the end of the year, there were five vehicles in the fleet, some of which bore names instead of the more usual fleet numbers. The Ellesmere Port route was extended to Birkenhead's New Ferry tram terminus in 1913 and this marked the company's entry into Merseyside which was to become the company's principal source of revenue, enabling the thinner operations in North Wales which, generally speaking, were profitable only in summer, to be cross-subsidised throughout the year.

Despite wartime restrictions, the company established itself in Crewe and Nantwich and its services reached out to Market Drayton, Whitchurch and an armaments factory at Queensferry. In 1919 new routes were quickly established between Chester and Warrington, Runcorn, Mold, Flint and Holywell and these territories and Merseyside were consolidated over the next 4-5 years. From 1924-25, the company's tentacles penetrated deeply into North and Central Wales, to some extent by the acquisition of existing operators. Crosland-Taylor snr died in 1923 and management passed to his second son, Claude.

In August 1928, the four main line railway companies who had been losing traffic, both passenger and goods, to road since 1919, obtained Parliamentary powers to operate road transport services and there was great apprehension among road transport operators. However the railway companies ran buses in very few cases and exercised their powers by buying shareholdings in existing bus companies or purchasing whole companies outright. A final offer of 27/6d (£1.3700) per share was made for Crosville by the London, Midland and Scottish Railway Company and accepted on 5th February 1929 after a full day of bargaining. Crosville shares were quoted on the Liverpool Stock Exchange at 26/- and the final offer was considered fair but not generous.

The railway company took over on 1st May 1929 but Crosville retained its identity, managed by the Crosland-Taylors as railway employees. Railway money was used to buy several businesses in North Wales and in some cases far too much was paid. The unproductive capital became a heavy burden on the company which had consistently paid a dividend of 10% during the 'twenties.

The railways soon concluded a far-reaching agreement with the Tilling and BAT bus holding groups covering the shareholding in bus companies country-wide and a new company, Crosville Motor Services Ltd. with LMS, Tilling and British Automobile Traction shareholding was registered on 15th May 1930, ending one year of outright railway ownership. It was railway initiative which led to the establishment of sound working relationships in Liverpool and Birkenhead. There was a further change from 1st May 1933 when the Western Transport Co. Ltd. of Wrexham (which had absorbed the Great Western Railway bus services in 1930) was taken over and part of the railway shareholding was then held by the GWR. Claude Crosland-Taylor became general manager of the new company but he died suddenly, aged 45, on 31st March 1935, management being assumed after an interval by his younger brother W.J. (James) who held the office until his retirement.

During the 'thirties, the company's fleet more than trebled from 300 at the time of the LMS purchase to just over 1000 at the outbreak of war and dividends crept back up from 4% to 8%. Much of the traffic was seasonal and the company fought hard for every hundredth of a penny per mile of profit. Sometimes money was saved by running acquired vehicles in the liveries of their previous owners until a repaint was really necessary and eschewing such luxuries as destination blinds, using the quaint Widd plates – a paper label sandwiched between two sheets of celluloid – to indicate the route being operated.

Reorganisation

From 1st January 1942, the BET and Tilling Groups simplified their financial structures resulting in certain bus companies being transferred from one Group to the other. Crosville, a company which had always had a distinctly BET outlook, became a Tilling company and was subject to that Group's policies which were much more centralised. Thus standard liveries, either red or green, and fleet policies favouring Bristol chassis and Eastern Coach Works bodies were applied and Crosville opted to become a green company, though wartime restrictions delayed the full implementation of the livery change from the maroon which dated from the brief period of LMS ownership.

Post-war Tilling body designs incorporated large destination and intermediate route indicator displays with route numbers and Crosville, which had never indulged in such luxuries, was obliged to conform. Route numbers, allotted on an area basis, first appeared in May 1946 and initially they included a wide range of suffix letters which were abruptly abandoned when buses with three-column number blinds were introduced. The resultant chaotic numbering system (with 29 variations of route 1 in Wirral!) was tolerated until the whole system was renumbered with area prefix-lettered numbers in July 1959.

From 1st January 1948, the railway shareholding passed to the newly-formed British Transport Commission and later the same year, the Tilling Group, anticipating nationalisation under the provisions of the Transport Act 1947, sold its interest voluntarily to the Commission so that Crosville, in company with all the other Tilling companies, became 100% state-owned. The government wisely decided that the bus companies should retain their management structures and function in a commercial manner and the company continued in this way for the next twenty years experiencing the post-war traffic boom until about 1950 and then the slow decline as television and private transport changed social habits.

Throughout these changes, management remained in the hands of the founding Crosland-Taylor family until 31st December 1959 when W.J. retired; he died, aged 73, on 4th October 1967. No other Tilling Group company could claim such a record of continuous management.

When the Merseyside PTE unified ownership of local transport on both sides of the river from 1st December 1969, the fate of Crosville was in the balance. Many bus services in the sparsely populated Welsh districts were cross-subsidised by Merseyside operations and the company could not remain viable without them. However, from 31st January 1972, both Crosville and Ribble became agents of the PTE and, with certain modifications, the *status quo* on Merseyside was maintained until Deregulation Day, 26th October 1986.

Meanwhile, by direction of the Secretary of State for Transport, Crosville had been split on 10th August 1986 into two companies, Crosville and Crosville Wales.

The break-up of the company in 1990, as described in Chapter 9, was a melancholy conclusion to a remarkable story of both private and public enterprise, spanning over 80 crowded years. Those who knew the company in its heyday will remember the clock-like precision of the pre-war Crosville buses and the immaculate turnout of the grey and green coaches. The contribution made by the company to the economic development of Merseyside and North Wales and, some would say, to the colonisation of Liverpool by the Welsh, is indisputable. Even in the austere days of Freddie Wood's chairmanship of the NBC, Crosville was always different. Its early struggles for hundredths of pennies a mile had fine-tuned its commercial instincts and produced the innovative machine seen at its best in the late 'forties when a host of second-hand vehicles was turned into a very effective fleet. Now Crosville has fallen victim to the social changes of the times and while the name lives on, the charisma of the lost original has gone for ever.

A group of 11 mainly Daimler buses lined up at a government factory at Queensferry during the 1914-18 war. This was an important source of revenue and enabled expansion to get underway once peace returned.

CHAPTER 1
WIRRAL FOUNDATIONS

The success of Crosville's Chester-Ellesmere Port service was due to a great extent to the inconvenience of the roundabout railway route which always involved a change of trains at Hooton. During 1910 the company had bought at auction a Herald charabanc, of French manufacture which had previously been used by the Pontardawe Motor Co., and a Germaine wagonette of unknown origin. Both were worn out and the service was started with an Albion charabanc bought in Liverpool.

From 25th January 1913, some trips on the Chester-Ellesmere Port route were extended via Rivacre, Hooton Park, Eastham and Bromborough to New Ferry tram terminus where passengers could catch Birkenhead Corporation trams for Woodside. A Daimler CC, probably a manufacturer's demonstrator, (*Flying Fox*), a Lacre (*Grey Knight*) and three Daimler CDs, one of which was named *Busy Bee* were added to the fleet. No more buses were named. The Lacres and Daimlers continued to run for many years. *Alma* (FM 387), a Dennis, ran between Charing Cross and Seacombe for the Birkenhead and Seacombe Omnibus Co after sale in 1918. Another Dennis had been named *Deva*.

The Germaine wagonette seen in the Crane Wharf workshop.

The Royal George, Lacre No. FM 469 (later No. 3), was photographed leaving New Ferry Toll Bar on the first day of the Chester - New Ferry service, 25th January 1913.

The new service was properly licensed by Chester City, Wirral Rural District and Lower Bebington Urban District Councils and was an immediate success. In a letter dated 1st September 1913 from Claude Crosland-Taylor to the Town Clerk of Birkenhead, seeking permission to extend the service to Woodside, it was stated that 60,000 passengers had been carried and a local service was already being run on Saturday evenings between New Ferry and Bromborough. The direct service along the main road through Great Sutton, Little Sutton and Childer Thornton had already been started, probably in early summer, and fares were quoted from New Ferry to Bromborough (3d), Eastham (5d), Little Sutton (8d) and Chester (1/3d). Although the company did not wish to carry local traffic between New Ferry and Woodside, licences to operate into Birkenhead were refused and the outbreak of war a few months later prevented any further steps being taken for some years. Many bus services ceased

The Royal George was one of seven named buses in the Crosville fleet before the 1914-18 War and the first new Lacre. Registered FM 469, it was new in 1912 and had an open rear platform, Paris-style; it continued in service until about 1923 by which time it had lost its name and had been numbered 3. The toplights, probably in ruby glass, have been used to advertise the company's activities - 'Cars and Commercial Vehicles, Repairs and Accessories, Tyres, Petrol and Oils'. In the lower view it is seen in Bromborough village on the New Ferry-Chester service on which it ran the first journey as shown on page 6.

The Leyland C7 was the last type of bonneted full size bus to be added to the Crosville fleet, No.164 being one of three (163-5) to enter service, mainly for longer interurban routes, in 1925. Note the roof luggage rack and the ladder at the rear. It was powered by the same 36hp engine as the G and SG types but was designed with a lightweight frame so that it could be fitted with pneumatic tyres. The C7s were withdrawn along with the other mid-'twenties buses in 1932.

because their vehicles were commandeered by the army but Crosville seems to have escaped, possibly because they ran services to a munitions factory at Queensferry. The direct service was suspended but the route through Ellesmere Port to New Ferry was continued.

By the end of the war, Crosville was ready to expand in Wirral and North Wales. While Wirral was much more populous than many rural areas, the company's strategy was aimed at tapping Liverpool's teeming thousands. This necessitated getting buses down to Woodside ferry or establishing convenient connections with the Mersey Railway. Birkenhead Corporation was equally determined to keep Crosville at bay and to develop a network of bus services of its own, an ambition so far thwarted by the War.

In March 1919, Crosville approached the Lower Bebington Urban District Council for permission to establish a daily local service between New Ferry, Bromborough and Eastham which was granted with the proviso that some trips should run through Lower Bebington Village and Port Sunlight. This would have involved the use of Lever Brothers' private roads and, after almost a year of negotiations, permission to use Wood Street was withheld. The service along the main road was introduced giving, with through buses to Ellesmere Port and Chester, a frequency of 15-20 minutes throughout the day.

Sir William Lever

In the meantime, a few services had been established in Wirral by other operators. In June 1914 a service was inaugurated by Sir William Lever between Prenton tram terminus, at the corner of Storeton Road and Prenton Road West, and Raby via Thornton Hough with a view to providing some form of transport for the residents on the extensive Lever estates in the area. There were two buses, a Star and an Alldays and Onions, each seating between 20 and 26 passengers. The buses used several private roads on the Lever estate. Sir William, later Lord Leverhulme, had offered these roads to the Rural District Council but they had declined to adopt them so the gates were kept locked and the conductors had to unlock and re-lock each gate as the bus passed through.

The service continued during the war with women drivers and youths as conductors but it is known that the buses were also used to convey workers between New Ferry tram terminus and the Lever factories at Bromborough Port and it was probably this activity which enabled a petrol ration to be obtained.

The women drivers were trained and the buses maintained by Joseph Forsyth who, in the 1970's as a nonagenarian, was still living in New Ferry Road, near the Great Eastern Hotel. Mr. Forsyth provides an interesting link with this period as, in 1919, he bought a 14-seater Crossley bus and tried unsuccessfully to obtain a licence for a service between New Ferry and Eastham. He went into partnership with a Mr. Simpson in a garage and taxi business at 8 New Ferry Road and used the Crossley for private hire work. It was eventually sold to J. Bell of Moreton about 1921.

Onward to West Kirby

Later in 1919, Crosville proposed to start a New Ferry-West Kirby service running via Lower Bebington, Clatterbridge, Thornton Hough, Brimstage and Heswall and, on hearing that Cheshire County Council had agreed to this on payment of 3d per mile towards road maintenance, Lower Bebington Council agreed to it on similar terms. These charges by road authorities were a feature of bus operation at this time and applied to all services started after 1916; they were a severe burden to bus proprietors, necessitating relatively high fares being charged. They disappeared with the passing of the Roads Act, 1920 which established the Road Fund, financed by licence fees, from

Alldays and Onions Ltd. was not a well-known manufacturer of buses and, as far as is known, William Lever was the only Merseyside bus operator to run one. The vehicle carries a board for the route between Prenton tram terminus, Birkenhead and Raby.

which grants for road maintenance and improvements were made to local road authorities. Nevertheless, operators were frequently inveigled into making special payments for specific road works in return for the granting of licences. Crosville paid £3,000 towards the improvement of the Upton-Moreton road, £500 for widening Mount Road between Borough Road and Storeton Road and later contributed £1,140 towards the cost of strengthening Meols railway bridge.

The New Ferry-West Kirby service started about 1st October 1919 and Lower Bebington's mileage payment for the first quarter was £19-2-1d.

These services were at first worked from Chester, but this soon became uneconomic and, before long, one or two buses were being kept overnight in the yard of the Great Eastern Hotel, New Ferry. Joe Forsyth carried out basic maintenance work and when his business fell on hard times in 1922, Crosville acquired Simpson and Forsyth's premises on the south side of New Ferry Road, near the Toll Bar. The building was extended forward to the building line and developed as a combined depot and bus station. Joe Forsyth joined Birkenhead Corporation as a mechanic and his son was later employed in a similar capacity.

Municipal Aspirations

In the north-east corner of Wirral there were two substantial municipal tramway operators – Birkenhead and Wallasey – and by 1914 both tramway systems were at maximum mileage. In 1910 Birkenhead had appointed a dynamic manager named Cyril Clarke who recognised the commercial potential of the motor bus. No doubt he had seen the Crosville company's buses at New Ferry and urged his Committee to persuade the Watch Committee to refuse licences to run through to Woodside for which the company applied in September 1913. He also persuaded the Town Clerk and the Council that the Corporation needed statutory powers to run motor buses to feed the tramways with passengers from outlying districts and block further attempts by private enterprise to establish bus routes. He had visions of municipal buses penetrating to all parts of the Wirral peninsula.

The Birkenhead Corporation Bill, deposited in November 1913 provoked seven petitions, one of which was by Crosville though most were presented by road authorities and railway companies who were seeking safeguards for their own interests. However, by the time the Bill reached the Commons, agreement had been reached with all accept the Wirral Railway who feared competition to Bidston and Moreton. Wallasey was concerned that Birkenhead might be in a position to block its own expansionist ambitions in the future. Lower Bebington and Bromborough Council objected outright but if granted, reserved the right to veto bye-laws and inspect the buses. There were to be no overhead wires and it also reserved the right to run its own buses and trams!

The Birkenhead Corporation Act 1914 received the Royal Assent on 31st July 1914 only five days before the outbreak of war. It allowed Corporation buses to run anywhere within the borough and on six routes outside its

Traffic on new routes was often worked up with small capacity buses. No.85 was one of four 30hp Leyland A7s added to the fleet in 1923. It was a shortened version of the G7 with a length of only 19ft 1in and seated 20 passengers. They were fitted with pneumatic tyres quite early and ran until 1931, having been renumbered 101-4 in the meantime. The small buses were ideal for routes such as Chester-Ellesmere Port via Wervin and Stanney where the roads were narrow and the Heswall-Banks Road local with steep hills and light traffic.

boundaries, subject to the consent of the various local authorities. These routes extended to Moreton Cross via Bidston; Upton Village; along Storeton Road from Prenton tram terminus to a point near Lever Causeway; Woodchurch (Horse and Jockey) – the later site of the Arrowe Park Hotel; Port Sunlight via Old Chester Road and Greendale Road and then via Bolton Road and New Chester Road to New Ferry; from the boundary near New Ferry to Bromborough Cross

Wallasey's ambitions were protected by a clause which provided that should Wallasey introduce a Bill for powers to run buses in Moreton and a portion of the parish of Bidston, Birkenhead would not oppose the application if the powers sought were similar to those granted in the Act. Even in 1914, Wallascy had its eyes on Leasowe and Moreton as the only areas into which it could expand.

The Corporation brought a London General B-type double-decker to Birkenhead and members of the Council went on an outing to Moreton on the eve of the 1914-18 War which then delayed any progress being made for five years.

Wallasey, whose expansion was restricted by water on three sides of the borough, had more limited ambitions. Powers to run buses had been rather half-heartedly sought in 1908 in connection with a tramway extension Bill which failed but in 1920 the Council thought it prudent to seek powers to run within the borough and outside in the only direction available – to the west – before Birkenhead scooped the pool. The external routes were to Leasowe and Moreton (then outside the borough); Upton, Hoylake and West Kirby and from Leasowe to the Birkenhead boundary at Bidston. In the teeth of objections from road authorities, the powers granted by the Wallasey Corporation Act, 1920 were restricted to operation within the borough.

C.F. Rymer

The Quality Motor Garages, an associate of the Quality Coal Co. of New Brighton, experimented with motor buses from 1915 and, with the war at an end, registered a new company, C.F. Rymer Ltd., on 26th March 1919. The man behind all these enterprises was Clarence Frederick Rymer, an outspoken extrovert, who had served on Wallasey Town Council as an Independent since before the 1914-18 War. An accountant by profession, he participated in several bus and coach ventures, none of which were particularly successful.

In 1919 he proposed a network of bus services in North Wirral based on Wallasey which resembled very closely what was eventually established by Crosville. Licences were refused by Wallasey Licensing Justices and a brief period of illegal operation between Wallasey Village and West Kirby ensued, mainly at weekends. After threats of prosecution he concentrated on coaching, though some buses were run in Litherland and Crosby later in the 'twenties; he prospered for about twelve years until he was caught up in the bankruptcies of Gilford Motors and Lewis and Crabtree, the Heywood bodybuilders.

Leyland named this body type the 'Crosville' as, originally it was peculiar to the company. This was the SG7 long-wheelbase model with 27ft 6in long body and seating 40 passengers. Note the front axle, set back to get a better weight distribution; the front wheels were smaller to make steering easier. Nos.81-2 (FM 2366/65) entered service in 1922, being followed by three more (101-3) the following year and seven (121-7) in 1924. They were renumbered 99-100 in 1929. All these vehicles were fitted with pneumatic tyres and continued in service until 1931-2..

The first Dennis bus in the Crosville fleet (FM 387) was new in 1911 and before the name The Alma, subsequently being numbered 2, then 4. Its body was built by Henry Eaton of Manchester. It was sold in 1919 to the Birkenhead Motor Works who used it on a service between Charing Cross, Birkenhead and Seacombe Ferry for about two years.

Crosville Steps In

The refusal of Parliament to grant powers to Wallasey Corporation to run buses to West Kirby prompted Crosville to use West Kirby as a base for the development of services in North Wirral on similar lines to Rymer's proposals. On 11th May 1920 Crosville applied to Wallasey for licences to run to both Seacombe and New Brighton ferries; these were refused but permission was granted to run to Wallasey Village. A formal Agreement was drawn up under the terms of which the company agreed to pay £150 per year towards the upkeep of the roads.

David Randall who had worked for Crosville at Nantwich prior to army service in the 1914-18 War, started up the West Kirby operation and wrote his own account in a letter to the author as follows:-

'I went with the two buses, two 26-seater Daimler CK type on solid tyres (Nos.40 and 41 I think) from Chester the evening before we started this service which was either late June or early July 1920. The buses were kept at a garage at the corner of Bridge Road, West Kirby where I had a sort of office for cash and stores etc. A third bus was later added. West Kirby-Birkenhead (Waterworks, Upton Road) via Frankby and Greasby followed later that year and was much better than Wallasey in winter but the other way round in summer'.

The Wallasey route was soon extended 200 yards or so up St. John's Road to meet the trams at St. George's Road on 28th July 1920 according to a leaflet, but possibly a little later. In his last letter to the author a few weeks before his death, aged 91, in 1986, Randall recalled that during the winter of 1920-21 traffic was so sparse that the service was virtually run in two parts, Wallasey-Moreton Cross and Meols-West Kirby with through trips only at the start and finish of the day and to facilitate crew reliefs.

Birkenhead offered a better prospect than Wallasey for all the year round traffic but licences to run to Park Station were refused by the Birkenhead Watch Committee. Undaunted, the company started the service between West Kirby and the Birkenhead boundary at Bidston Hill Waterworks on 29th October 1920. A more unsuitable terminus – bleak, exposed and at the top of a long, steep hill – can hardly be imagined, but absurdities of this kind were not uncommon when there was a conflict of interests between municipal and private operators. Nevertheless, people used the buses as there was no railway anywhere near Frankby and Greasby.

In the meantime, on 14th July 1920, Birkenhead Corporation had started an approximately hourly service between Charing Cross and Upton via Park Station and extended it to Central Station a month later. Clarke was angry at having competition when his Upton service had been running for only three months and he met Crosland-Taylor and suggested that the company service should terminate at Upton from where the Corporation buses would provide a connecting service. Crosland-Taylor refused and started to run the buses down the hill to the tram route at Claughton Village which they could do unlicensed so long as the same passenger was not both picked up and set down within the borough. The bus then returned empty to the Waterworks at the corner of Boundary Road as fare paying passengers could not be picked up in Birkenhead.

By early 1921, six or seven buses were based at Smith's Garage, Bridge Road, West Kirby and several new services were introduced. The 'Wirral Inner Circle' linked West Kirby with Meols, Moreton, Upton, Greasby and Frankby, and back to West Kirby via Black Horse Hill, but this was not well-patronised and was abandoned after a short period of operation. The 'Wirral Outer Circle' was more successful and ran from West Kirby via Thurstaston, Heswall, Barnston, Woodchurch, Upton and Moreton to Wallasey Village from where the buses returned to Moreton and back to West Kirby via Meols and Hoylake. The round trip took two hours and there were four trips daily in each direction and an extra late one at weekends. There were also some trips from Wallasey to Claughton Village via Moreton and

Upton but these were short-lived. By August 1921, therefore, Crosville was serving the following routes in Wirral:-

Chester-New Ferry via the main road (about 2-hourly)
Chester-New Ferry via Whitby, Ellesmere Port and Hooton Park (8-11 trips)
Eastham-Bromborough-New Ferry (every 15-20 minutes)
Meols-New Ferry via West Kirby, Heswall and Clatterbridge (4-6 trips)
West Kirby-Wallasey Village via Moreton and Leasowe (hourly)
Wirral Outer Circle (4-5 trips in each direction)
Wallasey Village-Claughton Village (6-7 trips)
West Kirby-Claughton Village via Newton, Frankby, Greasby and Upton (10-13 trips)

In 1921, Randall left Crosville to start his own business based on Ormskirk, and the West Kirby operations were taken over by H.H. Merchant who was destined to assume control of all Crosville's Wirral and Lancashire operations until eventually becoming Traffic Manager before he was appointed General Manager of the erstwhile Caledonian Omnibus Co. in 1947. He retired to West Kirby in 1967.

Wirral Consolidation

Meanwhile, the company was suffering competition from J.M. Hudson who started running in September 1919 between Chester and Ellesmere Port with an ex-RAF Crossley bus. At first he was not licensed in Chester and loaded on private land adjoining the Coach and Horses in the Market Square but eventually Chester issued licences and competition became fierce. Hudson pioneered an alternative route through Upton, Stanney and Stoak with extra trips between Chester and Upton on Saturdays. Crosville cut fares in 1921 and painted a bus blue to resemble Hudson's but, after a period of racing and dangerous driving, Ellesmere Port Council told both operators that unless they came to some agreement, they would cancel both operators' licences. Hudson's business was taken over on 27th January 1922 and Joe Hudson joined Crosville as private hire manager.

The year 1922 was one of gradual expansion. Early in the year, a twice-daily service started between Chester and West Kirby, mostly along the main road but with a diversion from the Shrewsbury Arms, Hinderton to Neston, a double run to Parkgate and back, rejoining the main road at Five Lane Ends. From 1st July two more journeys were added, running via Puddington, Burton, Ness, Neston, Parkgate esplanade and Boathouse Lane. A local service was run between Meols and Heswall and some trips went through Caldy village. In October 1922 the Wirral Outer Circle, which had been worked in sections during the previous winter, was curtailed as a Wallasey-Heswall service as the remaining section was adequately served by the new routes.

One can speculate that plans were being made to extend buses from New Ferry Toll Bar down to New Ferry Pier from where Birkenhead Corporation ran a half-hourly ferry service to Liverpool, calling at Rock Ferry. However, several spans of the 1000ft. long pier were carried away in fog by a Dutch coaster in January 1922 and the ferry service was curtailed at Rock Ferry. Use of this ferry would have avoided licensing problems with Birkenhead for, although the pier itself was in Birkenhead, the approach roads were in Lower Bebington Council's area. New Ferry would never have been an adequate substitute for Woodside as the approach roads were narrow and the ferry service was suspended whenever there was fog. The summer route between Rock Ferry Pier and Raby Mere, a licence for which was refused by Birkenhead in March 1922, was almost certainly originally planned to run from New Ferry Pier.

The year 1922 also saw the start of two years of combat between the company and Birkenhead Corporation. An appeal by the company to the Ministry of Transport against refusal of licences to enable buses to pick up passengers for West Kirby at Claughton Village was successful and an increased service was put on with many buses running from Meols through Hoylake and West Kirby to Claughton Village. Three stands were allocated in Park Road West.

A permanent depot to hold 27 buses was opened in Orrysdale Road, West Kirby in 1923 and the first link

In the pioneer days, many operators were obliged to have a Dirty Tricks department to combat competition and this ex-Royal Flying Corps Crossley 'Tender J', was one of eight purchased in 1922 for chasing on such routes as Ellesmere Port-Chester. Not all carried fleet numbers but this one was No. 4 and remained in the fleet until about 1925.

between two parts of the company's growing empire was inaugurated in May of that year. This was initially a summer limited stop route with three trips daily between New Ferry and Mold. A route between Neston and New Ferry via Hinderton, Willaston, Hooton Green and Eastham, for which a fare list had been published in 1922, did not start as far as can be ascertained. It appeared also in a fare list dated 1st January 1923 together with a route from New Ferry to Parkgate via Thornton Hough, Five Lane Ends and Neston of which there is no firm evidence.

In the 1923 Session, Birkenhead Corporation promoted a Parliamentary Bill which included a clause seeking authority to run buses anywhere outside the borough with the approval of the Minister of Transport. Crosville petitioned Parliament and the clause was defeated. In January, the company started a new service of four trips a day between West Kirby and Claughton Village via Meols, Garden Hey Road, Saughall Massie and Upton, as a means of linking Hoylake directly with Birkenhead. The Corporation, perhaps sensing that all-out opposition would be petty, wrote to the company pointing out that the service was unlicensed and Crosville actually suspended the service for a time, presumably as a conciliatory move while other matters were afoot. In March the Corporation was informed by the company that they intended running buses between Heswall and Claughton Village via Thurstaston, Irby and Upton or via Lower Caldy Cross Roads, Frankby and Greasby. There was to be a minimum fare of 5d between Birkenhead and Upton to placate the Corporation. Later correspondence makes it clear that this service was run for a few weekends in 1923. These services were officially approved by the Watch Committee on 4th July 1923 provided that not more than three buses were to stand simultaneously in Park Road West, with a 10 yards gap between them, and Crosville withdrew an appeal they had submitted because of continual delay in dealing with their applications.

In May and June 1923, Crosville applied to Birkenhead for numerous new licences. All services, except West Kirby, terminating at New Ferry Toll Bar were to be extended to Woodside including new routes being planned from Parkgate and North Wales; the West Kirby-Claughton Village services were to continue to Park Station and Woodside and also to Central Station via Park Road West and Charing Cross and an additional service added via Moreton. The company offered to charge higher fares than the Corporation – 2d more to Park Station and 3d to Woodside. New routes were proposed between New Ferry and Moreton via Lower and Higher Bebington, Mount Road, Storeton Road, Woodchurch and Upton and Rock Ferry Pier and Raby Mere via New Ferry, Lower Bebington, Spital and Bromborough. The New Ferry-Moreton route entered the borough for only about 100 yards near the Half Way House. The company had intended to avoid even this brief incursion by running along Waterpark Road but the road was unsuitable.

On the Raby Mere route the company proposed to pick up in the borough only at Rock Ferry Pier and to charge double the Corporation fare between the pier and Bebington Station. Only part of the Eastham and Bromborough local service would be extended and if the New Ferry boats were reinstated, part of the service, both local and through, would go to the Pier instead of Woodside. The company proposed to charge double the tram fare between New Ferry and Woodside and hand over half the proceeds to the Corporation if the journey was wholly within the borough (the 'Birmingham conditions' – see below).

The Corporation regarded these applications with considerable alarm and procrastinated to the extent that Crosville interpreted their inaction as a refusal and appealed to the Ministry of Transport. They had, however, considerable support in local commercial circles and the Birkenhead Traders' Association wrote to the Town Clerk in July, urging the granting of licences to important shopping centres rather than to the railway and ferry exits.

Having asked the Ministry to defer hearing the appeal, the Corporation appointed a special sub-committee of the Watch Committee which showed great confidence in the chief officers by delegating negotiations to the Chief Constable and the Tramways Manager. In many towns, this sort of discussion was conducted by councillors with no technical knowledge. On the Crosville side the negotiators

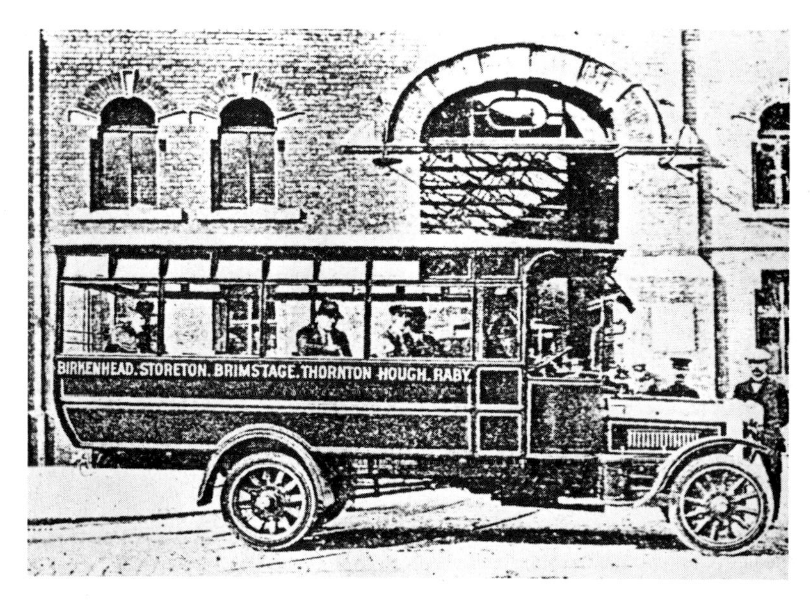

Lever's Star bus is seen outside New Ferry Tram Depot on a 1914-18 War workmen's trip to Bromborough Port Margarine Works (Planters), quite unrelated to the route board it displays. Levers ran a private train from Port Sunlight station at the main starting and finishing times and the bus appears to have been used for shift workers and maintenance men who worked different hours.

Four Leyland G7 buses, Nos. 63-66, being delivered on trade plates in 1922, show 'Chester direct', 'Chester via E. Port', 'Hoylake West Kirby' and 'Nantwich only' on their destination blinds. They were eventually fitted with pneumatic tyres and were withdrawn in 1928.

were Claude and W.J. (James) Crosland-Taylor and H.H. Merchant. A series of meetings was held in September and October during which the company's case seemed to be strengthened by the disclosure at a Municipal Tramways Association Conference in Portsmouth that the Ministry's policy was to allow private buses to penetrate to town centres with protective conditions for local tramway and bus services.

To protect their interests, the Corporation started a daily service between Woodside and Moreton Cross on 16th September 1923 and, about the same time, it seems that some journeys between Central Station and Upton were diverted via Park Roads South and West. No formal evidence of this has been found but the January 1924 time table shows no timing point at Park Station on these trips. They were presumably discontinued soon afterwards when the Crosville agreement was settled.

The Corporation took a census at New Ferry and found that Crosville was already carrying more than 500,000 passengers per annum on this group of services, a considerable number of whom started or finished their journeys by Corporation tram. Loss of only half the number would, it was estimated, cost £3,125 per year in lost revenue. This kind of development had been going on throughout the country and in some towns the local authority had already come to terms with company operators. During the Birkenhead discussions, various precedents were examined against local conditions. The 'Birmingham formula' actually allowed passengers to be carried wholly inside the city at double fare with half the revenue handed over to the tramways, a device calculated not only to discourage local travel on company buses but one in which the tramways could not lose if passengers chose to use the more expensive facility. Nearer home, the 'Warrington formula' allowed local travel with a 3d minimum fare of which $1^1/_2$d was handed over to the tramways. The 'Widnes formula' prohibited the picking up or setting down of local passengers less than half a mile beyond the outer Corporation bus termini.

In Birkenhead, there was a mixture of different operating conditions. On New Chester Road the Corporation had statutory powers to run to Bromborough but the local Council would not allow them to do so and the Minister of Transport had dismissed their Appeal to him in 1923. Both Corporation and Crosville were running to Upton, the company with a voluntary fare of 1d more than the Corporation. The company's Moreton services ran only to Wallasey, whereas the Corporation had been running from Rock Ferry Pier, through central Birkenhead to Moreton since 1919.

The company rejected a Corporation suggestion that passengers should change from a Crosville to a Corporation bus and vice versa at Moreton Cross with through tickets between West Kirby, Hoylake etc. and Birkenhead issued by both operators. There was also disagreement about the picking up limit beyond New Ferry; the Corporation wanted Bromborough Pool Lane whereas Crosville insisted that it must have Bolton Road which would have given the company access to the Port Sunlight works traffic. In this case the company proposed to charge 4d to Woodside and was prepared to pay 3d over to the Corporation. As Cyril Clarke pointed out in a report, this was likely to be a

Daimler CK No. 27 appears to have met with a mishap. It was originally No. 9 and its body is so similar to that of AEC No. 27 pictured on page 95 that it seems likely that the body was transferred when the AEC was withdrawn, taking the fleet number with it. This view clearly shows the very narrow front wheels and the high floor level.

the company could say:-

'We collect £8,333 in fares and perform all the services in carrying these passengers and are only allowed to retain for ourselves £2,083 whilst the Corporation, who do nothing, receive £6,250'.

By early November the company had agreed to accept the 'Widnes conditions' on all the West Kirby-Park Station or Woodside services thus giving up their existing Birkenhead to Upton traffic and conceding complete protection to the Corporation on the Moreton route. The first setting down points were to be at Bermuda Road on the Moreton route, Overchurch Road on the Saughall Massie route and the bridge over the Arrowe Brook on the Frankby route. The '1d more' fare formula would also have applied. The exception was that when the Corporation was running less frequently than half-hourly on the Upton route, Crosville would have free trade. In practice this was in the mornings and after 8.0pm. On the New Ferry routes, a modification of the 'Warrington conditions' would have been applied, the Corporation receiving from the company the tram fare for the length of journey within the borough. The Bolton Road business was unresolved. The New Ferry-Moreton and Rock Ferry-Raby Mere routes were not regarded as contentious. The Corporation's inspectors were to have the right to inspect tickets and waybills on Crosville buses in the borough and only closed buses, not charabancs, were to be used except perhaps on the Raby Mere service.

On 22nd November Clarke met an official of the Ministry of Transport and on his return reported as follows:-

'....he made it quite clear that their policy was to allow outside buses into Towns and Cities, the only limitation being to require outside buses to charge a minimum fare of one penny more than the tram fare for passengers picked up or set down within the Borough Boundary. I put to him the question as to whether they would interfere with any agreement mutually arrived at between the company and the Corporation and he said 'No'.

'It appears that your Committee have, under existing conditions, no option but to grant the licences and, if the Crosville Co. will agree to the suggested conditions arranged between themselves, the Chief Constable and myself, these are much more favourable to the Corporation than you could hope to get if the Ministry of Transport were called on to deal with the matter'.

The Police went so far as to draw up a schedule of suggested routes for Crosville buses within the borough and, in a confidential report, Clarke pointed out that the grant of these licences to Crosville would inevitably be followed by like applications from Pye, Johnston and Richardson and would severely damage the businesses of the local coach excursion operators who were allowed to stand at Woodside for limited periods.

John Pye

Meanwhile, in the closing months of 1923, there was an unexpected development which was to change Crosville's progress in Wirral for the next few years, when the business of John Pye of Heswall came on the market. The company had been casting envious eyes on the substantial all-the-year-round business between Heswall and Birkenhead for some time and their brief weekend operations between Heswall and Claughton Village and the proposed service between Parkgate and New Ferry had been a ploy to put pressure on Pye.

The origins of Pye's bus service between Heswall and Birkenhead have not been determined accurately but various oblique references suggest that it started about 1916, a strange time in view of the wartime petrol restrictions. It is possible that Pye, like Crosville, was in some way involved with serving the munitions factory at Queensferry but this is pure conjecture. At that time, Heswall was a large village divided into two parts, the old part or 'Lower Village' and the newer part stretching along Telegraph Road, the main road between Chester and West Kirby. The railway station was situated on the river bank about a mile from Telegraph Road and travel to Birkenhead by rail involved a circuitous journey via Parkgate and Hooton. It was therefore fertile ground for the motor bus.

John Pye's bus business grew out of his main activity as a motor dealer and taxi operator carried on from premises on the main road just south of the Cross. Once the war was over, the support given to it by the Heswall people persuaded Pye's uncle to put up capital for expansion and the original route through Pensby was increased in frequency and some trips were run through Thurstaston and Irby. About November 1921, a third route, via Barnston was added and by the summer of 1922 there was approximately a combined half-hourly service.

Birkenhead Corporation would not allow the buses to run to Woodside and licences were issued only to the corner of Singleton Avenue and Borough Road where connection was made with the trams on the Prenton route. Pye eventually built a bus station and waiting room there; two buses could stand off the highway and two more were tolerated at the kerbside.

A separate service was started between Parkgate and Prenton Tram Terminus via Thornton Hough and Clatterbridge, partially covering the same route as Lever's buses which had ceased running in 1918. The Parkgate bus was not permitted to run to Singleton Avenue. This route did not cross the borough boundary so its buses did not need to be licensed in Birkenhead.

Even with the change to and from trams, the Heswall buses gave the public a more frequent and convenient route to Woodside than the railway and a very large proportion of the Heswall-Birkenhead traffic was soon being carried by Pye's buses. Despite the business brought to their trams, Birkenhead Corporation were hostile to Pye. His licences were endorsed: 'Special Conditions. No passenger to be set down outwards within six miles of borough boundary and vice versa. Restricted to Woodchurch Road and Singleton Avenue'. As Heswall itself was less than six miles away, the condition was obviously absurd.

On 13th June 1923, Pye applied for six additional licences as his existing eight were insufficient to meet the demand, particularly at summer weekends. The Chief Constable recommended that they be refused as 'buses stand too close to the corner now. Rear of first bus should be in line with tree outside shop'. Refused they were but only a month later an additional licence for a charabanc was granted to J.G. Richardson of Southdale Road, Rock Ferry who had run a bus to Heswall via Irby seasonally from a stand at Elmswood Road since 1921-22, with a few summer journeys to Thurstaston Shore. He eventually concentrated on private hire and excursions. It is believed that this business passed to Charles H. Williams who operated from Southdale Road during the 'thirties and was taken over by Crosville on 22nd July 1937.

E.& J. Johnston, (trading as Borough Motor Works), of 474 Borough Road also ran a regular, if infrequent, service from a yard in Carlton Road to Heswall by way of both Pensby and Thurstaston using a Leyland charabanc and a Daimler 20-seat bus. His application for additional licences was also approved.

Pye took legal advice and about August 1923 started to run buses down to Woodside Ferry in the mornings, returning between 5.0 and 6.30pm. Advantage was taken of a loophole in the legislation whereas a bus was not deemed to be plying for hire unless a fare was taken on board. These through buses were available only to contract (season ticket) holders or people with books of prepaid tickets. These buses were immensely popular; they covered virtually every road of importance in Heswall and there were through trips from Banks Road, near the railway station.

Pye's No.8 was an Albion 20-seater, chassis No. 30091, new in 1919. Four buses, a charabanc and a lorry of this marque passed from Pye to Crosville in January 1924. Pye's livery is believed to have been silver grey.

By 1923 Pye owned about 20 vehicles of various makes – Straker Squire, Albion, Pagefield, Fiat, Bristol, Tilling Stevens, Ford, Dodge and GMC. All ran on solid tyres and six of them were charabancs. He also ran another charabanc and taxi business at Rhos-on-Sea, founded about 1922, but the two fleets seem to have been kept separate. The shadowy uncle in the background was now urging him to sell.

There has been speculation that Birkenhead's policy towards Pye was influenced by Clarke's ambition for the Corporation to purchase the business, although additional Parliamentary powers would have been needed. It was about this time that Crosville started negotiating with Pye and it can be assumed that Claude Crosland Taylor had been trying to alarm Pye to persuade him to sell by such tactics as running between Heswall and Claughton Village at weekends.

On 9th November 1923, John Pye wrote to the Town Clerk as follows:-

'Dear Sir,

'I do again make application for two more licences to ply for hire at Singleton Avenue, Birkenhead. I cannot understand why your Committee continually turn my applications down and grant opposition firms as many as they require. I was first to run a service of Busses (sic) from Heswall to Singleton Avenue, B'head; the others came later and do not run a regular service. I am a ratepayer in Birkenhead and also employ 8 Birkenhead men. I have always tried to work with B'head Corporation in many ways. They have forced me to run contractors' buses from Woodside because it was impossible to carry them from Singleton Avenue with the licensed buses we have. Now the Crosville Company inform me today that you have practically agreed to allow them to run buses from West Kirby and New Ferry to and from Woodside. I think if a bus service is allowed to run to Woodside, Heswall should come first. We have 200 Contractors, Business People. Heswall train service is bad and a long way round. West Kirby have a good train service and run direct. Hoping you will deal fairer with me.

'Yours Obediently
'John Pye'.

Pye agreed to sell the Heswall business, including a valuable plot of land in the centre of the town, to Crosville for £25,000-£17,500 in cash and £7,500 in shares. It has been said that the deal was actually struck on 7th November in which case it seems possible that Crosland-Taylor put Pye up to writing the letter. If, in fact, the deal was finalised later, it was perhaps an attempt to increase the value of the business before the sale. The truth will probably never be known.

Crosville applied to Birkenhead for the transfer of the licences and for additional licences. This was opposed by excursion operators Harding's, Macdonald and Co. and W.B. Horn Ltd in what appear to have been co-ordinated letters, all dated 27th December 1923 and also by Borough Motor Works two days later. All the applications went to the full Watch Committee and the Council and by 8th January 1924 when heads of agreement were set down, the broad negotiation picture had changed radically.

The First Birkenhead Agreement

The company had been induced to drop its New Ferry-Woodside application *in toto* in return for agreement on a Park Station terminus for the West Kirby services, the Woodside and Central Station extensions being refused. The picking up limits previously agreed (the 'Widnes conditions') were confirmed including the Upton exception, an empty concession, as the Corporation were soon running half-hourly at all times. Licences were granted for the New Ferry-Moreton and Rock Ferry-Raby Mere services. In the final Agreement, Crosville also voluntarily forfeited their right of appeal to the Minister of Transport.

In view of Clarke's November report, what happened to enable the Corporation to assert its authority in this way? The working papers for the final phase of the negotiations have not come to light if, indeed, they ever existed. The opposition of the local operators could have been given some weight as they included some influential men. Congestion at Woodside was another factor. Crosville had estimated a need for 60 licences for the New Ferry and West Kirby extensions and undertook to restrict the number of buses standing to six. But the deciding factor almost certainly lay in the deal with John Pye. It was probably made clear to Crosville that the satisfactory transfer of the licences was dependent on the company being 'reasonable' in other matters. Difficulties could be made to arise in connection with the Singleton Avenue stands as the Chief Constable had previously complained about obstruction. There was also the very important matter of additional licences to enable the service to be developed.

As it was, the same draft agreement promised the company 'full facilities at Singleton Avenue, that is to say, will license as many Buses as the Company require....' The company agreed to find room for two buses to stand on their own premises at 2-4 Singleton Avenue but retained the right to stand two buses on the roadway. A new route was granted between Rock Ferry Pier and Heswall via Storeton. This was much better treatment than Pye had received.

While Pye's services with half a million passengers annually were an attractive financial proposition, access to Woodside from New Ferry would have brought not only the population of Birkenhead but Liverpool's half million within reach. The Crosville management seem to have been unaware of the Ministry's policy though Clarke told his Committee that he had seen a copy of a trade journal containing an article on the subject in the company's head office! The most likely explanation is that, having agreed to pay Pye mainly in cash, the company had serious cash flow problems. The Heswall traffic was worth much more than the New Ferry traffic in winter and they could not risk difficulties with the licence transfer. The Liverpool traffic therefore had to wait. If they could have held out they would almost certainly have got their buses to Woodside in 1924 and probably from Singleton Avenue too. This was a major reverse for Crosville and if the Pye deal had come a year earlier or later, events might have taken a different course.

Pye's business was taken over by Crosville on 22nd January 1924 (backdated to 1st) and the first formal agreement between Birkenhead Corporation and the company, giving effect to the above, was signed on 26th February 1924. John Pye then concentrated on the Colwyn Bay business which was run by the family until 1965. Two of his sons went to work for Birkenhead Corporation; one became a timekeeper at New Ferry depot and the elder, Albert, was killed when a land mine demolished an air raid shelter at Laird Street depot in March 1941.

Crosville took over 13 buses, six charabancs and an Albion lorry from Pye together with a valuable plot of land near the centre of Heswall. A garage and bus station was built and it is reasonably certain that Heswall had the first purpose-built bus station in the north of England. Pye Road still runs through the site nearly 70 years later. The 20 vehicles were valued at £8,950, so £16,050 was paid for land and goodwill. It is not certain if all 20 vehicles were runners. Crosville added a 'P' to the Pye fleet numbers on several of them but most were sold during 1924. A few were permanently numbered and retained for a year or two.

County Borough of Birkenhead.

OMNIBUSES, WAGGONETTES, & OTHER CARRIAGES.

CARRIAGE LICENSE.

No. 121
M.A. 9642

The Mayor, Aldermen and Burgesses of the Borough of Birkenhead acting by the Council of the said Borough, under and by virtue of the provisions of the Town Police Clauses Act, 1847, the Public Health Act, 1875, and the Birkenhead Corporation Act, 1881, and in pursuance of a requisition duly made to them in accordance with the said Acts, DO HEREBY LICENSE a four wheeled Carriage, commonly called an Omnibus to ply for hire as a Motor Hackney Carriage within the limits of the Borough of Birkenhead, from the 16th day of July 1923 until the First day of July, 1924, under and subject to the Orders, Rules, Regulations, and Bye-laws respecting Omnibuses, Waggonettes, and other Carriages, and the Proprietors and Drivers thereof, from time to time in force, and to the statutes in that behalf made and provided, and to the special conditions on back hereof.

Name or Names of Proprietor or Part Proprietor of the Hackney Carriage	Place or Places of Abode.
John Pye	Heswall

Given under the Common Seal of the said Mayor, Aldermen and Burgesses this 15th day of Septr. 1923

Sealed in the presence of

Mayor.

(This License must be delivered up to the Inspector of Hackney Carriages on the Annual Inspection Day).

437-829 250 11-20.

A copy of the hackney carriage licence issued by Birkenhead Watch Committee for Pye's Straker Squire bus No. 5, (previously No. 10) MA 9642. The special conditions on the back precluded the setting down of passengers within a six-mile limit, well beyond the Heswall terminus!

PYE'S MOTOR & OMNIBUS COMPANY

JOHN PYE, PROPRIETOR.
Telephone - 108 Heswall.

TELEGRAPH ROAD,
HESWALL.

PETROL, OIL, GREASE, TYRES, AND ALL ACCESSORIES STOCKED. EVERY DESCRIPTION OF MOTORS AND TAXIS FOR HIRE.
ORDERS PUNCTUALLY ATTENDED TO.

9/11/23

Dear Sir

I do again make application for Two more License to ply for Hire at Singleton Avenue Birkenhead, I cannot understand why Your Committee continually turn my applications down & grant opposition Firms as many as they require, I was first to run a service of Buses from Heswall to Singleton Avenue Bhead. the others came later & do not run a regular service I am a rate payer in Birkenhead & also employ 8 Birkenhead men I have always tried to work with Bhead. Corporation in many ways, They have forced me to run contractors Buses from Woodside because it was impossible to carry them from Singleton Avenue at times with the Licence Buses we have. —
Now the Crosville Company informe me to day that you have practically agreed to allow them to run Buses from Ch. Kirby & New Ferry to & from Woodside Ferry. — I think if a Bus service

A copy of the first page of John Pye's letter written to the Town Clerk, Birkenhead on 9th November 1923, complaining of poor treatment by the Watch Committee. The bus depicted is a Straker Squire of which there were five in the fleet.

CHAPTER 2

CONSOLIDATION IN BIRKENHEAD

During the first months of 1924, the ex-Pye services were carried on much as before though the grant of additional licences enabled the traffic to expand, particularly in the summer months. The new service between Rock Ferry Pier and Heswall via Storeton and Barnston started in time for Easter, on 9th April, with 5-7 trips daily at intervals of 2-3 hours but it never assumed any importance. It was to be Storeton's only bus service, its only other link with the outside world being the LNER trains between Seacombe and Wrexham.

Pye's Parkgate service from Prenton tram terminus was continued and the route via Thornton Hough was supplemented by an additional summer route through Raby Village, Willaston, Hadlow Road, Burton and Ness. The contractors' buses to Woodside prospered and many of them served roads in Heswall which were not covered by the ordinary services. For the winter of 1924-25 there were 13 morning trips between Heswall and Woodside; by May 1928 there were 27 plus two early runs to Central Station only probably thus truncated in order to get the buses back to Heswall in time to do another journey at the height of the peak demand. Five through journeys ran seven days a week. Some trips were obviously designed for shoppers as the last departures from Heswall arrived at Woodside at 11.10 and 11.20am. Perhaps to ease traffic congestion in Borough Road, the Chief Constable decreed that, in the mornings, the buses should run via Woodchurch Road, Ridley Street, Westbourne Road, Eastbourne Road, Claughton Road and Hamilton Street but on the return journeys they were allowed to use Chester Street, Market Place South and Borough Road. Ordinary fare paying passengers could be carried as far as Balls Road on the inward journeys. The views of the residents of Ridley Street about this procession of buses down their narrow residential street from 7.45 each morning are not recorded. Another opportunity exploited from the summer of 1924 was the provision of an 'on demand' service at fine weekends between Singleton Avenue and Thurstaston; charabancs were often used to carry this traffic.

Meanwhile, on 12th March 1924 the West Kirby-Claughton Village services were extended to Park Station and the new service via Moreton started. Stands were allocated in Beckwith Street on the east side of Duke Street and for many years, buses unloaded at the station entrance, turned right into Beckwith Street, reversed near St. Anne's Church and moved forward on to the stand, leaving via Beckwith Street and Cavendish Street. The move to another stand in Beckwith Street, west of Duke Street, which eliminated reversing and the need for passengers from the trains to cross the road, was more than ten years in the future. Initially, each service ran hourly with peak hour extras on the Moreton route and a half-hourly service on the Frankby route after 12 noon on Saturdays and Sundays. Many journeys were linked as a circular, maintaining the facilities provided by extending the Frankby buses to Meols. The Saughall Massie route now had only 4-5 trips a day. No buses ran on any route on Sunday mornings. New cheap return fares (e.g. West Kirby-Park Station 1/3d), books of 12 tickets sold at discount rates and £1 monthly contracts were offered and there is no doubt that the Wirral line railway traffic was seriously affected especially from 1925 when Crosville and the Mersey Railway collaborated to offer through tickets to Liverpool via Park Station.

Other new services were introduced in time for the 1924 summer season. New Ferry to Moreton Cross via Higher Bebington, Prenton and Woodchurch started on 21st May but never achieved its apparent potential. It was the first bus service in Higher Bebington and the only one to run along Village Road between Kings Road and Mount Road. The company's promise to pay for a 'danger post' at the top of Woodchurch Lane was duly carried out. Singleton Avenue to West Kirby via Irby Mill Hill and Grange (later diverted via Caldy) started a week later and Rock Ferry Pier to Raby Mere, a summer route, a week after that, this piecemeal progression being dictated by the delivery of new buses.

An unwelcome development on 1st October 1924 was the purchase of Johnston Bros. Heswall service by Alfred Harding of Charing Cross, an experienced charabanc operator, established as early as 1891. However, Mr. Harding agreed to sell his interest and Crosville's monopoly was achieved from 10th January 1925. The Watch Committee agreed to the use by Crosville of Johnstons' yard in Borough Road as a relief terminus. The Park Station and Singleton Avenue termini were also used to develop a network of seasonal services to North Wales.

Agreement with Wallasey

Territorially, Crosville achieved more in Wirral in 1924 than in any other year. But there were still some barriers to break down. In 1923, the company had unsuccessfully renewed its efforts to persuade Wallasey Corporation to allow buses to run to Seacombe, Egremont and New Brighton ferries but after an appeal to the Minister of Transport, a compromise was reached and, from 13th April 1925, Crosville buses were allowed to extend to the Queens

Crosville's combined bus station and garage in New Ferry Road, near the Toll Bar, about 1928 with Leyland Leviathan No.220 on the Bromborough local service and an unidentified single-deck bus. Note the comprehensive publicity signs listing all the main destinations served. The depot was used until March 1932 and was later converted to a market.

Singleton Avenue bus station about 1928 with Leyland Lion PLSC3 No.300 (later B75) and SG7 No.127, dating from 1924 and now fitted with pneumatic tyres. The difference in floor level of the two buses is clearly discernible. The Lion appears to be in the short-lived bright red livery belying the wrought-iron sign which reads 'Crosville Grey Motor Services'. A tram stop sign and feeder box can be seen to the right of the buses. Note that the drivers wore leggings and most of the staff are wearing their white summer cap covers, a common feature in those days.

The full-cab arrangement of the SG7 made engine maintenance difficult and, in 1924, Leyland brought out its successor, the SG9 to the same dimensions but with a 40hp engine and the half-cab layout which was to become standard for full-size buses for the next 25 years. No.161 was part of a large batch of 25 SG9s placed in service in 1924-25; the later models entered service with pneumatic tyres which had only just become available for such large vehicles. The saloon was divided into two compartments – smoking and non-smoking – and there was a rearward facing seat along the front bulkhead. Crosville took the last of the SGs to be built; all were sold in the massive exodus of obsolescent types in 1932.

Above: Daimler CK No.59 (formerly 100) was new in 1920 and gave 11 years service. In this picture, taken in Beckwith Street, near Park Station, about 1929, it is painted in the red livery and is working the West Kirby via Saughall Massie service. The rear step of a Leviathan double-deck bus can also be seen.

Right: A pocket time-table issued by Crosville for all services passing through Heswall nine months after the acquisition of J. Pye's services. Note that the Heswall terminus is already described as a 'bus station' though it is doubtful if all the buildings had been erected.

CROSVILLE
"GREY" MOTOR SERVICES

TIME TABLES

From October 1st, 1924, until further notice.

HESWALL CROSS BUS STATION
to
SINGLETON AVENUE BUS STATION, BIRKENHEAD,
Via
(1) PENSBY. (2) BARNSTON. (3) THURSTASTON.
also
Showing Contractors' Buses to and from Woodside.

HESWALL CROSS BUS STATION
to
ROCK FERRY PIER,
Via BARNSTON AND STORETON.

PARKGATE AND NESTON
to
PRENTON ROAD TRAM TERMINUS, BIRKENHEAD,
Via
(1) Thornton Hough. (2) Burton—Willaston—Raby.

HESWALL CROSS BUS STATION—MEOLS,
Via WEST KIRBY AND HOYLAKE.

CROSVILLE MOTOR CO. LTD.,
Heswall Cross Bus Station, Telegraph Road. Phone—280 Heswall.
5,000—1/10/24.

Arms Hotel, Liscard Village, a convenient point in a part of the town which eventually became the commercial centre. There were direct connections with three of the Corporation's four tram routes and one bus route so the company was in a strong position to develop their routes, particularly the 'main line' to West Kirby. An infrequent Liscard-Parkgate route via Moreton, Upton, Greasby, Thurstaston and Heswall was commenced that summer. There were also some Liscard-Upton trips, which did not thrive and were diverted to run between Moreton Shore and Upton in 1926.

On 15th February 1926, Crosville signed a formal agreement with Wallasey Corporation, fixing the first setting down point as half a mile beyond the limits of the Corporation's bus operations. This was initially at St. Nicholas Road with provision for a revision when Corporation services were extended to Moreton. A few months later, when Wallasey deposited a Bill in Parliament aimed at extending its boundaries, Crosville petitioned against it, withdrawing the Petition only when a formal Agreement had been made safeguarding the company's interests in Leasowe and Moreton. On 1st April 1928, the day Leasowe and Moreton were incorporated into the County Borough of Wallasey, the Crosville restriction point was moved to Leasowe Castle. Merchant, who had to deal with many local authorities on both sides of the Mersey, described Wallasey Council as the most intransigent of them all.

The framework of Crosville's Wirral network was now complete and the rest of the decade was spent in refining and consolidating it. The isolation of New Ferry on Sunday mornings when the trams did not run was alleviated by the Corporation allowing the 11.0am bus to Mold to load at Rock Ferry Pier on that day from Easter 1925 and, from April 1926, to meet public criticism, Sunday morning trams were run from Woodside to both New Ferry and Singleton Avenue.

A New Ferry-Eastham Ferry service started in 1925; the boats from Liverpool ran to Eastham until 1929 and the hotel and woods were still popular. The seasonal Prenton-Parkgate via Willaston service was diverted via Brimstage but the route was abandoned at the end of September 1926 in favour of a strengthening of the main service via Thornton Hough. The presence of the grey Crosville buses in the town centres was its own advertisement and traffic expanded rapidly. The Park Station-Moreton-West Kirby and Liscard-West Kirby services were running daily every 15 and 20 minutes respectively by the summer of 1928 – seven buses per hour between Moreton and Hoylake where eight years earlier there had been none.

Birkenhead Corporation Act, 1926

Birkenhead Corporation deposited another Bill in Parliament for the 1926 Session asking for powers to run buses anywhere within a five mile radius of Birkenhead Town Hall which would have cleared the way for Corporation buses to run to Clatterbridge, Eastham, Greasby, Pensby and Barnston. The company prepared a Petition and this

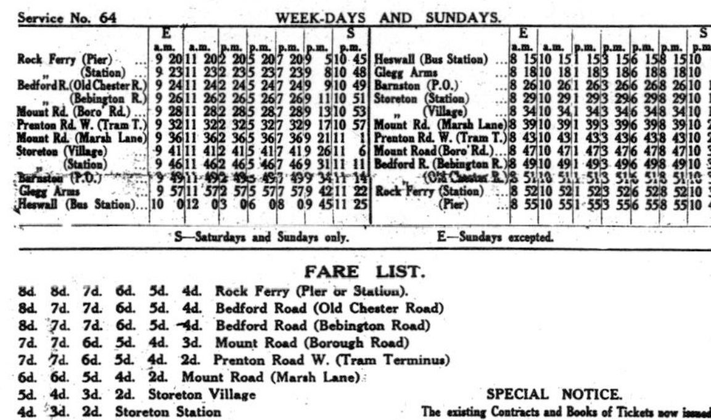

CROSVILLE

"GREY" MOTOR SERVICES

NEW SERVICE

ROCK FERRY (Pier) to HESWALL

(Via STORETON and BARNSTON)

Commencing Wednesday, April 9th, 1924,

TIME TABLE and FARES until further notice.

Service No. 64 — WEEK-DAYS AND SUNDAYS.

	E						S
	a.m.	a.m.	p.m.	p.m.	p.m.	p.m.	p.m.
Rock Ferry (Pier) ...	9 20	11 20	2 20	5 20	7 20	9 5	10 45
„ (Station) ...	9 23	11 23	2 23	5 23	7 23	9 8	10 48
Bedford R. (Old Chester R.)	9 24	11 24	2 24	5 24	7 24	9 9	10 49
„ (Bebington R.)	9 26	11 26	2 26	5 26	7 26	9 11	10 51
Mount Rd. (Boro' Rd.) ...	9 28	11 28	2 28	5 28	7 28	9 13	10 53
Prenton Rd. W. (Tram T.)	9 32	11 32	2 32	5 32	7 32	9 17	10 57
Mount Rd. (Marsh Lane)	9 36	11 36	2 36	5 36	7 36	9 21	11 1
Storeton (Village) ...	9 41	11 41	2 41	5 41	7 41	9 26	11 6
„ (Station) ...	9 46	11 46	2 46	5 46	7 46	9 31	11 11
Barnston (P.O.) ...	9 49	11 49	2 49	5 49	7 49	9 34	11 14
Glegg Arms ...	9 57	11 57	2 57	5 57	7 57	9 42	11 22
Heswall (Bus Station)...	10 0	12 0	3 0	6 0	8 0	9 45	11 25

	E						S
	a.m.	a.m.	p.m.	p.m.	p.m.	p.m.	p.m.
Heswall (Bus Station) ...	8 15	10 15	1 15	3 15	6 15	8 15	10 [illegible]
Glegg Arms ...	8 18	10 18	1 18	3 18	6 18	8 18	10 [illegible]
Barnston (P.O.) ...	8 26	10 26	1 26	3 26	6 26	8 26	10 [illegible]
Storeton (Station) ...	8 29	10 29	1 29	3 29	6 29	8 29	10 [illegible]
„ (Village) ...	8 34	10 34	1 34	3 34	6 34	8 34	10 [illegible]
Mount Rd. (Marsh Lane)	8 39	10 39	1 39	3 39	6 39	8 39	10 [illegible]
Prenton Rd. W. (Tram T.)	8 43	10 43	1 43	3 43	6 43	8 43	10 [illegible]
Mount Road (Boro' Rd.)...	8 47	10 47	1 47	3 47	6 47	8 47	10 [illegible]
Bedford R. (Bebington R.)	8 49	10 49	1 49	3 49	6 49	8 49	10 [illegible]
„ (Old Chester R.)	8 51	10 51	1 51	3 51	6 51	8 51	10 [illegible]
Rock Ferry (Station) ...	8 52	10 52	1 52	3 52	6 52	8 52	10 [illegible]
„ (Pier) ...	8 55	10 55	1 55	3 55	6 55	8 55	10 [illegible]

S—Saturdays and Sundays only. E—Sundays excepted.

FARE LIST.

8d. 8d. 7d. 6d. 5d. 4d. Rock Ferry (Pier or Station).
8d. 7d. 7d. 6d. 5d. 4d. Bedford Road (Old Chester Road)
8d. 7d. 7d. 6d. 5d. 4d. Bedford Road (Bebington Road)
7d. 7d. 6d. 5d. 4d. 3d. Mount Road (Borough Road)
7d. 7d. 6d. 5d. 4d. 2d. Prenton Road W. (Tram Terminus)
6d. 6d. 5d. 4d. 2d. Mount Road (Marsh Lane)
5d. 4d. 3d. 2d. Storeton Village
4d. 3d. 2d. Storeton Station
3d. 2d. Barnston (Post Office)
2d. Glegg Arms
Heswall (Bus Station)

SPECIAL NOTICE.

The existing Contracts and Books of Tickets now issued from Heswall and Barnston to Birkenhead will also be available from Heswall and Barnston to Rock Ferry as an alternative Route.

Special Conditions attached to this Service. The Company will not pick up or set down on this route within the Borough of Birkenhead, any person unless such person be travelling to or from or beyond a point at the junction of Mount Road with Marsh Lane, otherwise passengers may be picked up ANYWHERE and put down ANYWHERE in Birkenhead, and the following is the route which will be traversed :—Bedford Road, Bedford Avenue, Bedford Drive, Mount Road, Borough Road, Prenton Road West, Storeton Road

This service also passes Austin's Nurseries at Barnston.

Issued subject to the Company's terms, conditions, and regulations as set out in Main Guide.

Proprietors:—THE CROSVILLE MOTOR CO., LTD., Crane Wharf, Chester.

Tel. 1123 Chester (2 lines). Char-a-bancs and Motor Buses for Private Hire.

Local Office: TELEGRAPH ROAD, HESWALL. Telephone 108 Heswall.

5,000—9/4/24.

The announcement of the commencement of the Rock Ferry-Heswall service in April 1924. Note the title – Crosville 'Grey' Motor Services – used until 1929 and the typical upside-down fare table.

direct route via Woodchurch Road but wanted to be able to run from Moreton and Upton also. They also needed more powers to run in Bebington which was building up rapidly and they wanted to run further along Hoylake Road, Moreton and to the Shore.

Crosville's view was that expansion should be on a mutual basis and any further penetration into the Wirral by the Corporation should be achieved only at the expense of concessions in Birkenhead. In retrospect, this seems to have given the company an opportunity to pursue the extension of services to Woodside but it does not appear to have been done. The agreement reached, on the basis of which the company withdrew its Petition, was dated 15th March 1926 and allowed Birkenhead Corporation buses to run about half a mile further along Hoylake Road, Moreton to Bermuda Road but moved the restriction point for Crosville buses about 600 yards nearer to Birkenhead from Bermuda Road to Moreton Schools (effectively Rosslyn Drive). The Corporation could use the new alignment of Woodchurch Road instead of the old road nearer the village, but neither route to Arrowe Park could start until the estate had been purchased and was open for public use.

In Upton the restriction points for Crosville buses were moved eastward along Greasby Road about 300 yards from Arrowe Brook to Upton Cricket Ground and on Saughall Massie Road from Overchurch Road to the western end of the Convent wall, a concession of about half a mile on a largely unpopulated road. The Corporation was to repay to the company half the money paid to Wirral RDC in 1921 for widening the Upton-Moreton road. (The Corporation paid Crosville £2,060 on 28th September 1927).

Crosville buses on the Rock Ferry-Heswall service could use Mount Road between Borough Road and Storeton Road instead of diverting via Prenton Road West and Corporation buses could run on certain roads in Bebington and Bidston where there was no effective competition with the company.

The easing of restrictions on the Greasby and Saughall Massie routes had little practical value as the roads remained essentially rural in character for some years. However the Moreton concession was of considerable value as the district west of Moreton Cross was built up over the next few years and the Crosville service was regarded by many passengers as a superior limited stop facility between Park Station and the west end of Moreton. This was assisted by the introduction of cheap early morning fares from anywhere between Bermuda Road and Moreton Schools to Park Station at 2½d single and 5d return. Although there were no comparable fares on the Liscard route, after the Corporation buses started running to Moreton in April 1928, the Crosville service assumed a similar express status on that route also. The rapid progression of company buses along Laird Street and Hoylake Road, Birkenhead and Leasowe Road, Wallasey contrasted strongly with the pedestrian speed of the municipal buses.

In 1926 Crosville extended the New Ferry-Moreton Cross service to the Shore, bringing it into conflict with the last remaining local service operator in Wirral. This was Cole's 'Dinky Bus' who ran first a Ford model T and later a Vulcan, both 20-seaters, between Moreton Cross and the Shore during the twenties. Mr. Cole drove and collected the fares himself – 1d for adults and ½d for children. At fine summer weekends, Crosville ran a shuttle between the Cross and the Embankment with an open charabanc.

The moves made in Moreton by Birkenhead Corporation during 1927 and the early part of 1928 were essentially tactical as it was anxious to make its position secure before the district was absorbed into Wallasey on 1st April 1928 after which licences would be needed from Wallasey Watch Committee. As Wallasey had its own transport ambitions, Birkenhead might have had some difficulty in reaching its objectives. The Moreton services were extended from the Cross to Bermuda Road on 1st February 1927. A shuttle service using small buses commenced between the Cross and the Embankment in June, effectively putting Cole's Dinky Bus and Crosville's charabanc out of business. Pasture Road was in poor condition and the railway bridge at Moreton station was only half its later width. Following negotiations with Wirral RDC, the latter agreed to accept £600 towards the cost of strengthening the bridge to make it suitable for full size buses; it was not widened for several more years. A through service from Woodside to the Embankment started on 1st September 1927 and a second service between Upton and the Embankment, in direct

Cole's Ford Model T bus is seen in Pasture Road at Moreton Shore early in the 1920s.

it suitable for full size buses; it was not widened for several more years. A through service from Woodside to the Embankment started on 1st September 1927 and a second service between Upton and the Embankment, in direct competition with Crosville, followed on 1st January 1928. There was little demand, particularly in the winter. This was a direct challenge to the company which had been serving the Moreton Cross-Upton road since 1921. Both operators lost heavily and the Corporation, having established itself on the route, wisely withdrew the service for the winter on 25th October 1928.

It is believed that Birkenhead Corporation still had ambitions of reaching West Kirby but two influential residents who were substantial Crosville shareholders ensured that Hoylake UDC maintained the company's exclusivity.

Developments from New Ferry.

Further south, a local service between New Ferry and Spital Cross Roads (sometimes referred to as the Edgeworth Estate) was started by Crosville in 1927. These were short journeys on the Meols service. Early in 1929, Bebington Council asked Birkenhead Corporation to run buses between Woodside and Lower Bebington and a direct service via Old Chester Road started on 3rd March reducing the importance of the New Ferry route as passengers no longer changed to the trams or trains to get to Woodside.

Urban sprawl was spreading southwards, bringing more passengers to Crosville's New Ferry-Bromborough-Eastham buses. Some trips ran via Rake Lane, Eastham (now absorbed in the by-pass) and others ran via Lower Bebington and Trafalgar, bringing all the year round service to a road hitherto served only by the seasonal Raby

Leyland G7 No. 108, one of 10 placed in service in 1923, was originally numbered 103. It survived until 1931 and is shown in its final form with pneumatic tyres, all-maroon livery and the oval logo.

A view of New Ferry Toll Bar which symbolises the Great Divide between Birkenhead Corporation and Crosville which existed until 1930. On the left is tram No.8, originally a 1901 single decker which had been given a low height top deck suitable to pass under Chester Street railway bridge. On the right is a Crosville GH7 dating from 1924 which has just left the company's bus station in New Ferry Road.

All 12 of these massive Leyland Leviathan double deckers (Nos. 211-222) were based in Wirral, split between West Kirby and New Ferry depots. Birkenhead Corporation was also a major user of the type. They played an important part on the development of local traffic between West Kirby and Birkenhead and between New Ferry and Bromborough.

Mere route. The Stanlow oil installations justified a few workers' journeys by 1926. The route via Rossmore Road and Little Sutton became the main one and by the summer of 1928 there were only 5-6 trips a day via Hooton Park and a 30-60 minute frequency by the other route. The direct route via Great Sutton had a bus approximately every 90 minutes. New Ferry-Bromborough buses ran every 10-15 minutes with extras at peak hours including some workers' trips to or via Bromborough Port, a facility which prompted Lever Bros. to withdraw their passenger train service over their private sidings.

The Mold service was now extended along the Ruthin road to Loggerheads where, in order to stimulate the traffic, Crosville had bought the Tea House and some of the Leete Estate. The tiny public house 'We Three Loggerheads' had been popular from early in the century as the former London and North Western Railway had put on a bus service from Mold Station as long ago as 27th July 1908. This scenic spot drew crowds of Merseyside people and there was soon a bus every 30-45 minutes daily, with duplicates at weekends. Some buses ran express at a premium fare of 6d throughout and there were also some through trips from New Ferry to Pantymwyn.

When Crosville's West Kirby garage opened in 1923, 27 vehicles were based there but within six years the number had increased to 40 including coaches in summer. The depot accommodated only 32 vehicles and some buses were parked in Orrysdale Road and adjoining side streets and one or two at the railway station. Land was purchased on the east side of New Chester Road, near Woodward Road, Rock Ferry, in 1929 and plans were drawn up for a large new garage on the site.

The Railway Initiative

Following their acquisition of several provincial bus companies, approaches were also made by the railways to several municipalities and Birkenhead was agreeable to talks. The LMS wanted to get the Crosville services to Woodside, reasoning that this would result in an enormous increase in traffic and made its initial approach almost within days of taking over the bus company. The Corporation's view was now that expansion should be mutual; if Crosville buses were to penetrate to Birkenhead town centre then Corporation buses should push further into the Wirral villages to which many Birkenhead residents were already migrating. The Town Council, once more, wisely left the negotiations to the professionals, this time E.W. Tame, the Town Clerk and Cyril Clarke.

The first meeting took place on 31st May 1929; Crosville's team comprised Claude Crosland-Taylor, H.H. Merchant and Ashton Davies of the LMS. The Road Traffic Bill, which modernised the licensing system for buses, was in the offing and W.J. Crosland-Taylor, who took no part in the talks, maintained in his book that if Crosville had waited for it to become law, they would have been able to reach Woodside without surrendering valuable territory in return. The Corporation was anxious to finalise an agreement in time to submit a Parliamentary Bill in November 1929 as they knew that if they achieved their objectives, they would need further statutory powers. Contemporary Crosville people maintain that W.J's gloomy assessment of the outcome was the result of pique because Merchant and not he was selected as second negotiator. There is little doubt that the Road Traffic Act 1930 would have given Crosville access to Woodside from New Ferry, Singleton Avenue and Prenton but it is unlikely that they would have been able to establish the same long distance services, including the valuable routes to Caernarfon, which the agreement facilitated. Col. Sandeman Allan, MP is said to have advised Clarke to reach agreement quickly in case the Act enabled Crosville to get to Woodside without a *quid pro quo* for the Corporation. He seems to have done his homework and one wonders if the Crosville people had done theirs, particularly in view of the 1923 fiasco. On the other hand, the Crosville men were now railway employees and there may have been railway pressure behind the scenes as LMS over-eagerness caused many problems for Crosville not the least of which was over-capitalisation.

Draft agreements contained many clauses which did not find their way into the final version. A revenue and mileage pool was proposed for all the Birkenhead-Heswall services with 25% Corporation participation. Another clause foresaw Mersey Tunnel buses and suggested that if there were to be a Liverpool-Chester service, it should be shared as to one third by Birkenhead Corporation with provision for Chester Corporation to participate if they wished.

There is no doubt that Birkenhead knew exactly what they wanted and got most of it. The Crosville negotiators were shrewd enough to realise that suburban development would favour the direct Pensby road and refused to concede any rights there. Eventually, in order to avoid joint working on any route, the service via Irby and Thurstaston was surrendered. This had a heavy summer weekend traffic but there were also two rural miles which still remain largely undeveloped over half a century later. Agreement was reached in October, in time for the Corporation to submit their Bill.

In short, company buses were to be extended from New Ferry, Singleton Avenue and Prenton tram terminus to Woodside and Corporation buses were to be given access to Bromborough and Eastham; Irby, Thurstaston and Heswall; Greasby, Frankby and Thurstaston and Clatterbridge. Crosville buses were precluded from carrying local passengers between Woodside and Allport Road, Bromborough; Marsh Lane/Mount Road, Higher Bebington; Holm Lane, Woodchurch Road (or alternatively Ivy Cottage, Thingwall or Arrowe House Farm under certain conditions); Clatterbridge Workhouse (sic) on journeys via Lower Bebington (again, under certain conditions) and Landican Village in the event of a new road, then planned, being built. The revenue from the Eastham-New Ferry local service alone had exceeded £7,500 in 1928 so it was a high price that the company paid to get to Woodside.

There were a few exceptions. The New Ferry-Moreton Shore service was allowed to carry local traffic throughout (there was no other service to Higher Bebington at the time) and while the New Ferry-Meols buses could, in terms of the Agreement, carry no local passengers between New Ferry and Clatterbridge, this was suspended so long as the service did not exceed two buses per hour. There were a number of other provisions which will be discussed later.

The Birkenhead Corporation Act 1930 received the Royal Assent on 4th June and the Agreement with Crosville was signed two days later. Both Birkenhead Corporation transport undertaking and the new Crosville company were on the threshold of an era of enormous and exciting expansion.

Twenty-six Titan TD1s were taken into stock in 1931 of which L20 is seen in its immediate pre-war condition with destination blinds and smaller fleet title. It was probably fitted with he TD2 type radiator from new. Originally No.58, it was fitted with a diesel engine about 1944 when it became M170. It was withdrawn in 1953.

CHAPTER 3

THE LANCASHIRE SERVICES

In 1919 Crosville started new services between Chester and two important points on the higher reaches of the Mersey. These were quite literally on the river bank – the Transporter Bridge at Runcorn and Bridge Foot at Warrington. In due time, these became important and profitable routes in the Crosville network and, as Liverpool was a prime objective for expansion, the company's eyes not unnaturally turned to the Lancashire shore. It will become apparent that a great deal more effort was put into developing the Wirral network than to Lancashire and this may seem strange in view of the magnetic attraction of Liverpool. However, whereas the potential area to be tapped on the Cheshire side was virtually open-ended with the promise of two-way traffic, the area between Warrington and Liverpool was very firmly boxed in by well-established public transport facilities. Widnes, linked across the river with Runcorn by that ponderous contraption, the Transporter Bridge, had been one of the earliest municipal pioneers of the motor bus and served not only the town but all the principal north-south roads, including that to Rainhill on the main Liverpool-Warrington road, the present A57. From Rainhill, tramways led both north to St.Helens and west to Prescot and eventually Liverpool. Warrington had its own compact tramway and bus system which was contained within the borough boundary. East of the town, the Lancashire United company was well-established north of the river and the North Western company to the south. The limited territory available for expansion was mainly sparsely populated agricultural country so the company's scope was very restricted.

Liverpool's tramways extended to Garston, about half way to Widnes, and the City Council consistently refused to license any buses from out of town.

In 1921 Crosville was granted licences in Warrington for a service to Prescot via Bold Heath and Rainhill. It started about 1st October and ran about every three hours with a late bus at weekends. A formal agreement with Warrington Corporation was signed on 7th October, protecting the Sankey tram route but this was replaced by a new agreement on 1st January 1922 whereby Crosville charged a minimum fare of 3d (2d for children) and paid the Corporation 1½d per passenger (1d child) each quarter. It is not known how the service was worked initially but, in 1922, an out-station was opened at the Railway and Commercial Hotel Yard, Victoria Road, Widnes from which services were run from Widnes Town Hall to Garston (Island Road South) via Hale and Speke; Gateacre (Acrefield Road) via Hough Green and Tarbock Green and Warrington via Penketh. The exact commencing dates are

Leyland A7 No. 85 (later renumbered 101)) was new in 1923 and gave eight years' service, much of it on pneumatics. Buses of this type were based at the Widnes out-station to develop such services as Bowring Park to Prescot via Huyton Quarry, but they had long been relegated to duties in less populated areas before withdrawal.

unknown but Warrington Corporation agreed to the Widnes service in July. The Prescot service was then run from the Widnes base. Crosville agreed to give protection to a point half a mile beyond Widnes Corporation bus termini; no formal agreement was made, just an exchange of letters which was honoured until new conditions were negotiated in 1969.

The Gateacre service was poor as there was no direct connection to Liverpool and it was suspended in May 1923. In October of that year the Prescot-Huyton circular commenced running via Whiston, Huyton Quarry, Huyton Church and Huyton Lane and vice versa; in May 1924 it was running as a Prescot-Bowring Park tram terminus service with most journeys running only to St. John's Road corner via Huyton Quarry and less frequent services via Huyton Lane and also Cronton Avenue (Windy Arbour Road). This route had been run for a short time by Contour Motor Services whose proprietor was the same David Randall who had started Crosville's West Kirby operations in 1921. Alas, his business failed for lack of capital.

City Centre Reached

The original strategy visualised all the Widnes services converging on Garston but, if there was to be a tram journey, Wavertree, a shorter distance from the city centre, was seen as more favourable. As anticipated, Liverpool Watch Committee refused to issue licences to enable the Widnes-Garston service to reach the city centre and an appeal was made to the Ministry of Transport. Ribble, who

The 22hp Leyland Z5 was one of the smallest products of the manufacturer and the first to be fitted with pneumatic tyres as standard. No.120 was a one-off for Crosville and specifically designed for one-man operation. It is believed to have worked on the Prescot-Huyton services for a time. New in 1924, it was withdrawn from service in 1932.

Aintree tram terminus did the same. Both appeals were successful so stands were allocated at the Custom House, Canning Place, a bleak place with no shelter for waiting passengers. The Ribble service was extended on 8th April 1925 and it is believed that the Crosville-Widnes service reached Canning Place about the same time. A minimum fare of 6d was imposed for any journey starting or finishing within the city boundary and a circuitous route via Mossley Hill Road, Aigburth Hall Road, Aigburth Road, Princes Road, Canning Street and Duke Street was laid down by the Corporation. Nevertheless, the traffic increased rapidly and by 1926 the Warrington-Widnes and Widnes-Liverpool services had been linked as a through route. The route within the city was simplified a little, buses running via Bowden Road in lieu of Mossley Hill Road and Aigburth Hall Road.

The Garston service was at first run with Daimler CKs which were replaced by 36-seat Leyland SGs about 1924. In 1926-27, new PLSC Lions were put on the route in an attempt to run Pusill's Suburban Motor Service off the road. Pusill, who had started operations in 1919, ran between Penketh, Gt. Sankey and Warrington and was Crosville's only competitor in Lancashire. He enjoyed considerable local support and survived to sell out to Warrington

The Leyland PLSC Lion series with its low floor level, rendered many older types obsolescent, the first 10 (designated LSC1) entering service in 1926. The PLSC1 with its 14ft 6in wheelbase was soon succeeded by the PLSC3 model which, being 2ft longer, could seat up to 36 passengers. Number 64 of this type, shown in the red livery, was one of the last to be delivered, entering service in 1929 only a few months before the first LT1 Lions. It became B25 in the 1935 renumbering and ran until 1949. Note the absence of any destination equipment.

Corporation in February 1939.

The Tarbock Green route was reintroduced in 1926 running from Widnes to Wavertree Clock Tower via Gateacre, Woolton Road and Lance Lane with the usual 6d minimum fare within the city. There were frequent trams between Wavertree and the city and six trips a day were soon being run. A novel initiative was a summer route from Liverpool (Canning Place) to Loggerheads via Widnes Transporter Bridge, Runcorn, Chester and Mold, with connections for Ruthin and Denbigh. Leaving Liverpool at 9.45am, it arrived at Loggerheads at 1.15pm, returning at 6.35 and arriving back in Liverpool at 9.55pm. The return fare was 5/- (25p). This was a rare example of a service using the Transporter Bridge which was, of course, a novelty and timings were easy to allow for delay if the bridge car was full. The service prospered for five seasons and was eventually abandoned when it became much quicker to cross the river and travel from Woodside to Loggerheads.

New Depots

At the end of 1923, the company opened a garage in Chester New Road, Warrington and the Widnes yard was vacated. For about five years all the Lancashire services were run from Warrington though, as the Liverpool service built up it seems probable that one or two buses were out-stationed somewhere in the city. In 1927, a 3,350 sq. yd. site was bought at the junction of Church Road and Edge Lane and a typical Crosville depot of the period – steel framework with corrugated iron cladding – was built and brought into use in June 1928. It was extended in 1933 and adjoining land was bought in 1937; the maintenance facilities were extended in 1942.

From 1st June 1927 2-4 trips daily were run on an alternative route between Widnes and Wavertree, via Halebank, Halewood and Gateacre; this route was served on Saturdays and Sundays only in winter but daily in summer until 1930 when it became daily throughout the year. From 5th October 1927 the Warrington-Farnworth-Cronton-Wavertree service commenced with four trips daily but it was suspended after one year's operation. It appeared in the time table marked 'Discontinued Until Further Notice' for 11 years before it was reintroduced.

The value of a through service to the city centre had been well demonstrated by the success of the Warrington via Widnes service which, by 1928, was running half-hourly; two years later it was increased to every 20 minutes. The company, sensing a slightly more liberal policy towards outside buses on the part of Liverpool, applied to extend the Warrington-Prescot service to Liverpool and from 17th October 1928 it was allowed to terminate at the bottom of Mount Pleasant, opposite Lewis's and the Adelphi Hotel. The route was via East Prescot Road, Queens Drive, Edge Lane, Chatham Place and Oxford Street. As it passed the depot, crew changes could be done en route. Traffic immediately increased and within a year or two, the frequency of the through service was increased and some additional journeys were put on between Liverpool and Rainhill Stoops. A year later, the two Widnes-Wavertree services were extended via Wavertree Road and Botanic Road to Edge Lane depot but this did not last long as by early 1930 they, too, had reached Mount Pleasant.

Crosville, Lancashire United and North Western had agreed in the winter of 1928-29 to run an hourly joint express service between Liverpool and Manchester via Prescot, Warrington then alternately via Irlam and Eccles or via Lymm and Altrincham. Ribble had been running a service between Seaforth, Liverpool and Manchester between August and October 1928 but agreed to withdraw it as part of the rationalisation of company operating territories. On 9th March 1929, Crosville Leyland Lion No. 61 (later B22) was inspected by Manchester Watch Committee and duly licensed on 21st of that month. The other two operators began the service on 28th March with Crosville's blessing. Although the service was shown in the 1929 summer timetable, Crosville never actually ran though, in due course, it obtained a road service licence which it did not surrender until November 1934. If the company had participated, Crosville buses would have run four return trips per day and it was probably LMS control of the company that caused the change in policy. The joint operators agreed to protect local services of all three and from Liverpool no passenger was set down until reaching points east of Warrington and vice versa.

Agreement with Liverpool

No sooner had the LMS Railway brought the negotiations with Birkenhead Corporation to a conclusion than an approach was made to Liverpool Corporation with a view to establishing a similar concord. Here there was no dynamic local transport concern with a keen, progressive manager but a tramway-orientated undertaking with serious financial and logistic problems, headed by an ailing manager who was dominated by a headstrong and professionally incompetent Committee. Its attempts to establish a bus undertaking had been disastrous, the net effect being a draining of revenue from its own tramways. Unlicensed services were running into the city from Bootle and the whole undertaking was staggering towards dereliction.

Agreement was potentially more difficult as there were more parties involved. The LNE Railway Co., by virtue of its two-thirds interest in the Cheshire Lines Committee, claimed a place alongside the LMS and, in addition to railway-owned Crosville, there was Ribble Motor Services Ltd., in which the LMS obtained a substantial shareholding on 28th December 1929. That was the month in which the first meeting was held with Liverpool Corporation but it was not until March 1931 that agreement was reached. By this time Ribble had mopped up or gained control of the independent bus operators working into the city from the north, so there were fewer complications to an orderly settlement.

The first provisions of the Road Traffic Act, 1930 took effect in February 1931 and the Corporation was anxious for agreement, if only to protect its own interests. The Agreement was signed on 2nd July 1931, territorial interests

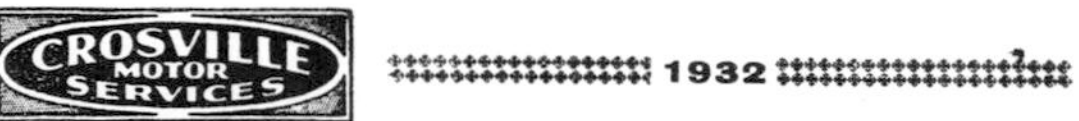

Liverpool (Pier Head)-Gateacre-Widnes

Via HALEWOOD and HALEBANK.

Commencing on Wednesday, February 24th, 1932, this Service will be extended to Liverpool (Pier Head).

Attention is called to the alteration of time-tables, fare-tables and routes, and conditions of picking up and setting down passengers in the City of Liverpool.

WEEKDAYS & SUNDAYS.

	R	R						
	a.m.	a.m.	a.m.	n.n.	p.m.	p.m.	p.m.	p.m.
Liverpool (Pier Head) ...	7 0	8 15	9 40	12 0	2 0	4 0	6 0	8 0
Liverpool (Mount Pleasant) ...	7 5	8 20	9 45	12 5	2 5	4 5	6 5	8 5
Wavertree Rd. (Tunnel Rd.)	7 10	8 25	9 50	1210	2 10	4 10	6 10	8 10
Wavertree (Clock Tower) ...	7 16	8 31	9 56	1216	2 16	4 16	6 16	8 16
Woolton Rd. (Cromptons Lne.)	7 20	8 35	10 0	1220	2 20	4 20	6 20	8 20
Woolton Road (Church Road)	7 24	8 39	10 1	1224	2 24	4 24	6 24	8 24
Halewood Rd. (Orient Drive)	[illegible]	[illegible]	[illegible]	[illegible]	[illegible]	[illegible]	[illegible]	[illegible]
Halewood (Gerrards Lane) ...	—	—	—	1229	2 29	4 29	6 29	8 29
Halewood (Derby Arms Hotel)	—	—	—	1232	2 32	4 32	6 32	8 32
Halebank Station	—	—	—	1236	2 36	4 36	6 36	8 36
Halebank (Beehive Hotel) ...	—	—	—	1239	2 39	4 39	6 39	8 39
Mersey View (Cock & Trumpet)	—	—	—	1241	2 41	4 41	6 41	8 41
Ditton Station	—	—	—	1244	2 44	4 44	6 44	8 44
Widnes (Town Hall Square)	—	—	—	1252	2 52	4 52	6 52	8 52

	R	R						X	P
	a.m.	a.m.	a.m.	p.m.	p.m.	p.m.	p.m.	p.m.	p.m.
Widnes (Town Hall Square)	—	—	—	1 0	3 0	5 0	7 0	9 0	9 30
Ditton Station	—	—	—	1 8	3 8	5 8	7 8	9 8	9 38
Mersey View (Cock & Trumpet)	—	—	—	1 11	3 11	5 11	7 11	9 11	9 41
Halebank (Beehive Hotel) ...	—	—	—	1 13	3 13	5 13	7 13	9 13	9 43
Halebank Station	—	—	—	1 16	3 16	5 16	7 16	9 16	9 46
Halewood (Derby Arms Hotel)	—	—	—	1 20	3 20	5 20	7 20	9 20	9 50
Halewood (Gerrards Lane) ...	—	—	—	1 23	3 23	5 23	7 23	9 23	[illegible]
Halewood Rd. (Orient Drive)	7 30	8 45	1010	1 25	3 25	5 25	7 25	9 25	9 55
Woolton Road (Church Road)	7 34	8 49	1014	1 28	3 28	5 28	7 28	9 28	9 58
Woolton Rd. (Cromptons Lne.)	7 38	8 53	1018	1 32	3 32	5 32	7 32	9 32	10 2
Wavertree (Clock Tower) ...	7 42	8 57	1022	1 36	3 36	5 36	7 36	9 36	10 6
Wavertree Rd. (Tunnel Rd.)	7 48	9 3	1028	1 42	3 42	5 42	7 42	9 42	1012
Liverpool (Mount Pleasant) ...	7 53	9 8	1033	1 47	3 47	5 47	7 47	9 47	1017
Liverpool (Pier Head) ...	7 58	9 13	1038	1 52	3 52	5 52	7 52	9 52	1022

R—Sundays Excepted. X—Saturdays and Sundays Excepted. P—Saturdays and Sundays Only.

SINGLE FARES.

1/- 11 10 9 8 7 6 5 5 4 4 4 Liverpool (Pier Head or Mt. Pleasant)
11 10 9 8 7 6 5 4 4 4 1 Wavertree Road (Tunnel Road)
10 9 8 7 6 5 4 3 2 1 Wavertree (Clock Tower)
9 8 7 6 5 4 3 2 1 Woolton Road (Green Lane or Cromptons Lane)
8 7 6 5 4 3 2 1 Woolton Road (Church Road)
7 6 5 4 3 2 1 Halewood Road (Orient Drive)
6 5 4 3 2 1 Halewood (Gerrards Lane)
5 4 3 2 1 Halewood (Derby Arms Hotel)
4 3 2 1 Halebank Station
3 2 1 Halebank (Beehive Hotel)
— — Mersey View (Cock and Trumpet)
— Ditton Station
Widnes (Town Hall Square)

RETURN FARES.

1/7 1/5 1/3 1/2 1/- 10 8 — — Liverpool (Pier Head or Mt. Pleasant)
1/4 1/2 1/- 11 9 7 — — Wavertree (Clock Tower)
1/1 — — — — — — Woolton Road (Church Road)
11 — — — — — Halewood Road (Orient Drive)
9 — — — — Halewood Road (Gerrards Lane)
7 — — — Halewood (Derby Arms Hotel)
6 — — Halebank Station
— — Halebank (Beehive Hotel)
— Mersey View (Cock and Trumpet)
Widnes (Town Hall Square)

SCHOOL CHILDREN'S FARES.

Special conditions for children travelling between **Liverpool (Pier Head) and Gateacre Station.**
Children under five years of age, free.
Children from five to fourteen years of age, half fare, also bona fide School children up to their 15th birthday (during term time only) and then only to and from School (Sundays excepted). Half 3d. fares, charge 1½d.; half 5d. fares, charge 2½d. In all other cases halfpennies treated as pennies.
For conditions between Gateacre Station and Widnes, see Company's Official Regulations.

Route in City of Liverpool:—Liverpool Pier Head (adjoining Cunard Buildings) James Street, Lord Street, Church Street, Elliott Street and Parker Street (Outward), (or Ranelagh Street (Inward), Lime Street, Mount Pleasant, Oxford Street, Chatham Place, Overbury Street, Wavertree Road, Picton Road, High Street, Church Road, Woolton Road, Gateacre Brow, Halewood Road, Lydiate Lane, Church Road, Halewood Village. Returning the reverse way.

PASSENGERS WILL BE PICKED UP AND SET DOWN IN LIVERPOOL AT ANY CORPORATION STOPPING PLACE.

Proprietors: CROSVILLE MOTOR SERVICES LIMITED, **Head Office, Crane** Wharf, Chester (Phone 2080).
5,000-2/32—S.G.M. Local Depot, Edge Lane, Liverpool (Phone, Old Swan 1308). City Office, 23, Water Street, Liverpool (Phone, Central 2604).

One of a series of handbills issued on the occasion of the extension of services to Liverpool Pier Head on 24th February 1932, a great day for the company.

Leyland Titan L61 was the first fully enclosed TD1 in the fleet, having been exhibited at the 1929 Commercial Motor Show with LMS-Crosville fleet name and fleet number 367. It is shown in Lord Street, Liverpool on the Pier Head-Mossley Hill-Garston service 'B', worked on behalf of Liverpool Corporation from 1932 to 1938. Note the two domes on the rear panel, indicating the division and depot to which the bus was allocated. This vehicle retained its petrol engine until withdrawn in 1952. The picture was taken in 1936 to show the effect of parked cars on public transport.

The 1934 double-deck order consisted of eight Titan TD3s with vacuum-hydraulic brakes with Leyland vee-front metal-framed bodies (916-23, M2-9 from 1935). Most of these buses were rebodied with Eastern Coach Works bodies in 1949-50 and remained in service until 1957-8.

Four Crosville buses stand outside the Dock Board building at Liverpool Pier Head in September 1937 with the Cunard and Royal Liver Buildings in the background. 1930 petrol-engined Leyland TD1 L24, destined for Warrington on the 'A' service is accompanied by 1936 TD4 M41 on service 'B' to Garston. M41 was the first Crosville bus to be bodied by Eastern Coach Works after its separation from Eastern Counties and is followed by a Lion LT2 of the D class, probably bound for Widnes and a 1935 V-front metal-framed Leyland-bodied TD4 bound for Prescot on the 'F' service via Huyton Quarry. In the background is a Liverpool Corporation AEC Regent and a Ribble Leyland PLSC Lion on Bootle services.

being defined in a manner common to several railway-inspired contemporary agreements. The inner or 'A' area was the responsibility of the Corporation; the middle or 'B' area, about three miles wide (but excluding Widnes and certain northern districts) was the joint responsibility of the Corporation and the companies, but the services were to be run by the latter, receipts and working expenses being apportioned; beyond this, the 'C' area, was exclusively company territory. Just outside the 'A' area was a 'Common Zone', up to half a mile wide which could be used by all parties to enable the Corporation to reach legitimate traffic objectives. The 'A' area included Speke which was not then within the city boundary. Tram services were excluded. The Prescot Road was designated the boundary between Crosville and Ribble but could be used by both.

There was to be a 4d minimum fare within the Corporation's area but this was not rigidly applied as the old 6d minimum had been and there were graduated fares near the area boundary. The Corporation received 30% of fares for journeys wholly within the 'A' zone, a heavy impost. The Agreement was fundamentally different from the Birkenhead one as there was no prohibition on the carriage of local traffic. A passenger could travel by Crosville bus within the city from one stop to the next provided the minimum fare of 4d was paid.

The New Network

In the south-east of Liverpool there were many Corporation services which were losing money heavily and, as the Road Traffic Act's licensing provisions were already in force, there was some delay while the necessary road service licences were obtained. The Corporation decided to withdraw a number of routes and let Crosville carry local passengers in the outer areas, particularly in Woolton, Gateacre and Hunts Cross. The revised network was introduced on 24th February 1932 when all the company's city services were extended to Pier Head from Canning Place or Mount Pleasant, back street routes being abandoned in favour of direct routes. The Warrington via Widnes service ran via Berry Street, Renshaw Street and Church Street while the Warrington via Prescot service, on which a Liverpool-Rainhill Stoops intermediate service was introduced, ran direct down Prescot Road, London Road and Dale Street. Both Widnes services were extended to the Pier Head via Church Street and some short journeys ran between Gateacre (Orient Drive) and Pier Head at busy times. A new service between Hunts Cross (The Grange), Woolton and Pier Head, with one journey extended from Halewood (Derby Arms), augmented the facilities in the Wavertree Road corridor. Suburban diversions such as Bowden Road, Garston and Lance Lane, Wavertree were abandoned in favour of direct routes and most services were accelerated. Some proposals which had been discussed were not adopted. These included the diversion of the Warrington via Prescot service via Eaton Road and West Derby Road and the Widnes services via Dunbabin Road and Ullet Road.

As part of its economy drive, the Corporation withdrawal of a Garston-Mossley Hill-Pier Head service in favour of a part-day route involving a change to and from trams at Aigburth, had been met with public dissatisfaction and Crosville was approached to provide a new service on behalf of the Corporation. Thus from 1st September the company started a service wholly within the city between Garston (Windfield Road) and Pier Head via Brodie Avenue, Dovedale Road, Crawford Avenue and Ullet Road. The service was instantly popular and the original 30-40 minute frequency was soon increased to about 20 minutes. Originally new TD2s 736-7 were dedicated to the service to be joined by AEC 'Q' 1000 in 1933.

The Liverpool network was completed on 26th July

1933 when the Prescot-Huyton-Bowring Park services were extended via Broad Green Road, Queens Drive, Childwall Road, Wavertree Road and Oxford Street to Pier Head with a basic half-hourly service. In their time tables Crosville insisted, for many years, on calling Childwall 'Wavertree (Garden Suburb)'. It was also of interest that in the publicity announcing the extension, reference was made to the Prescot-Huyton Circular even though there had been only one circular journey since 1924!

To assist in the identification of buses in Liverpool, a system of route letters was adopted from 17th June 1933 as follows:-

A	Liverpool-Warrington via Garston, Speke and Widnes
B	Pier Head-Garston via Brodie Avenue
C	Pier Head-Hunts Cross (or Halewood/Halebank) via Woolton
D	Pier Head-Widnes via Gateacre and Halewood
E	Pier Head-Widnes via Gateacre, Tarbock Green and Hough Green
F	Pier Head-Prescot via Huyton and Whiston
G	Liverpool-Warrington via Prescot and Rainhill
H	Liverpool-Rainhill Stoops via Prescot

Eventually as the service developed, F1 was allocated to the F journeys via Huyton Lane but the Cronton Avenue diversion continued to show the plain letter.

Extension of the services through the city streets to the Pier Head gave Crosville a much more visible presence in Liverpool which became an essentially double-deck depot, single-deck operation being mainly confined to the Widnes D and E routes. The route planning must have been right as there were virtually no changes in the network for over 20 years though there were several increases in frequency, as Liverpool's outer suburbs gradually extended. Many passengers would willingly pay 6d single or 11d return for a 35-minute ride on comfortable upholstered seats from Prescot to the Pier Head compared to 4d for a 51-minute tram ride on slatted wooden seats; Woolton took 27 minutes and cost 4d against 44 minutes (2d) on the tram. Liverpool Corporation buses maintained only a peak hour presence in Hunts Cross and had no all-day service to Speke until 1938. Crosville ran several short journeys to Dungeon Lane. The Corporation took back the Garston via Mossley Hill service from 11th October 1938 by which time a new Agreement had retrospectively reduced the toll to 15%, replaced the Common Zone by a number of designated common roads, abolished the B zone (except in parts of Ribble territory) and made each operator responsible for its own costs, thus simplifying clerical work. The Corporation was able to reach Huyton village, though by a different route, but the district was expanding rapidly and there was plenty of traffic for both.

In September 1938 the G & H service was given a basic half-hourly service to Rainhill with many trips extended to Bold Heath and from 22nd March 1939 the Wavertree-Warrington via Cronton and Farnworth service was reinstated after 11 years' suspension. It took the route letter K and terminated, as before, at Wavertree Clock Tower. There were three trips through to Warrington and eight to Farnworth, occupying one single-deck bus from 8.5am to 11.29pm. The A service was also increased, with a 15-20 minute service throughout.

There were few AECs in the Crosville fleet but this side-engined Q demonstrator AMD 256 was purchased in 1933, numbered 1000, and placed in service on the Liverpool-Garston route 'B' worked on behalf of Liverpool Corporation. It created an enormous impression in Liverpool's city streets among 25-year old trams and considerably enhanced the company's image. It finished its days at Rock Ferry in 1945 having become successively L87 and L68.

CHAPTER 4

WIRRAL IN THE THIRTIES

By 1930, the pioneering days of the bus business were over. For Crosville in Wirral there was the new Agreement with Birkenhead which, for better or for worse, would guide their fortunes over the next few years. There were new rules for everyone as the Road Traffic Act, 1930 was about to come into force. Apart from new regulations governing the construction and use of buses, the licensing of drivers and conductors and regular inspection of buses, the Act took away the licensing powers of local councils and vested them in new bodies of area Traffic Commissioners. Based in Manchester, the North West Commissioners had jurisdiction over a wide area of North West England and Wales and were responsible for approving routes, time tables and fares. Existing operators, including railway companies and local authorities were able to appear before the Commissioners and support or object to applications; there was a right of appeal against their decisions to the Minister of Transport. This procedure ensured that the same standards were applied throughout the region and local authorities could no longer frustrate the legitimate objectives of bus operators to protect their parochial interests.

The new laws were regarded with hostility and suspicion by many bus and coach operators, especially the smaller ones, and it was their inability to come to terms with the Act that led to a profusion of sell-outs to the larger operators during the 'thirties. Some proprietors, mainly in the coaching field, openly flouted the Act but most were very soon brought to book.

Implementation of the Agreement at Birkenhead predated the Act's provisions coming into force. Indeed, it was essential that it should, as later events indicate quite clearly that railway opposition would have frustrated many of the company's plans. Much midnight oil was burned in the preparation of new time and fare tables and duty schedules, new buses had to be purchased and arrangements made for their accommodation and maintenance and additional staff recruited and trained. New Ferry depot was hopelessly inadequate and whilst Crosville had bought land in New Chester Road, Rock Ferry in 1929, it was 1932 before the new depot built upon it was ready. For the time being, as many buses as possible were shedded at Heswall, West Kirby and Chester, resulting in some unproductive mileage.

The extension of services to Woodside took place in two stages, the first on 1st August 1930 when Crosville's Chester, Ellesmere Port and Loggerheads services were extended from New Ferry to Woodside. On the same day, Corporation buses started to run from Woodside to Eastham and from Upton to Bromborough Cross.

Crosville buses ran every hour on the Chester direct service, every half-hour to Chester via Ellesmere Port and a new service was started between Woodside and Ellesmere Port via Little Sutton and Pooltown Road, running roughly hourly in the morning and half-hourly in the afternoon. Six trips daily ran via Hooton Park and Rivacre. As events turned out, the Pooltown Road service was the only one on which the demand was over-estimated and the service was reduced in 1931. The strong Welsh influence within Crosville was subtly demonstrated by the inadvertent spelling of Rossmore Road as Rhosmore Road in the publicity matter!

A company bus leaving Woodside was not permitted to set down passengers before reaching Allport Road, Bromborough and there was free trade for Crosville and Corporation buses between there and Stanley Lane, Eastham

From 1931 legislation prevented one-man buses from having more than 20 seats and the Leyland Cub KP2 model was introduced in that year for use on lightly trafficked routes. Number N6 (originally 665) dates from two years later and was withdrawn in 1942 by which time there were few routes on which 20 seats were adequate.

Parkgate is a place where the tide rarely comes up but in this picture, 1934 Leyland Titan TD3 M6 with Eastern Counties body battles its way along the Esplanade on the service from Woodside in the teeth of a north-westerly gale. This was one of the first batch of diesel-engined double-deckers (M2-9). Note the fleet number position below the destination box which is still without a blind, a short-lived practice. After rebodying, M6 was withdrawn in 1956.

Moreton Station railway bridge before being widened in the late 'thirties with Leyland Lion LT7 H6 with 34-seat Leyland metal-framed body on the New Ferry-Moreton Shore service which was usually worked by a Leyland Cub. The small H class with only 15 vehicles was the last class of full size single-deck buses to be delivered new with petrol engines, some of the diesel LT7s (the J class) having already been placed in service when H6 arrived in 1935. Despite this, H6 remained on the road until 1951.

This fine view of Heswall depot and bus station dates from about 1945, shortly before the end of the war. Note the white paint on the offside mudguard of Leyland TD5 M77, designed to show up in the blackout but the headlamp masks have been removed as, by then, lighting restrictions had been eased. Leyland Titan TD1s made up the bulk of the depot's fleet and two can be seen together with 1934 Leyland Lion LT5A No. G17, the last of a small class of Lions. Each Lion model had its class letter though all the Tigers were classified 'K'. No. G17 was eventually fitted with a diesel engine, becoming GA17, and continued in service until the late 'fifties.

where the municipal buses terminated. The loss of local traffic was to some extent compensated by the acceleration of the services as the journey times between Woodside and Chester – 55 minutes direct and 1hr 10min via Ellesmere Port – were the same as those which had been allowed from New Ferry. On the outward journey, buses turned off the main road at the Toll Bar and called at the bus station in New Ferry Road as hitherto, a practice continued until the new depot opened on 1st April 1932.

A new service which had originally been proposed in 1922 and shelved, started on 1st October between Woodside and Burton, following the main Chester road to Hooton Cross Roads then through Willaston, Hadlow Road, Neston and Ness with a bus every 2-3 hours. Another new but infrequent service ran three times daily between Woodside and Holywell via Flint, a facility previously advertised by connections at Queensferry. This became express in 1931 but only 10 minutes were saved and it reverted to a stopping service in May 1933.

The second stage was effected on 1st October 1930 when all the Heswall-Singleton Avenue services were extended to Woodside via Borough Road, the route via Thurstaston and Irby being taken over by Corporation buses. In addition, the Parkgate service was diverted at Lever Causeway to run down Thornton Road and Borough Road to Woodside and the West Kirby-Singleton Avenue service was extended to Hoylake and Meols at one end and to Woodside at the other with a bus every two hours. Some changes were made to the New Chester Road services in the light of experience and the infrequent Woodside-Ellesmere Port via Hooton Park Gates service was linked with Chester-Ellesmere Port via Stoak and Stanney to give a third through route between Birkenhead and Chester using small one-man buses. When it became known, it was sometimes used by trippers whose return tickets were inter-available with the direct service.

The Parkgate service had a bus alternately every 30 and 60 minutes with every other bus diverting to pass the Shrewsbury Arms, Hinderton. The through journey took 39 minutes, only four minutes longer than the old route from Prenton Tram Terminus. The Heswall services were also speeded up; on the Pensby route the journey to Woodside was given the same time allowance as had been given to Singleton Avenue.

One facility lost to the Heswall business travellers was the almost door-to-door service they had enjoyed on the contractors' buses to and from Woodside. The Agreement forbade the placing in service of a new fleet of buses by either party without reference to the other so Crosville put new fully enclosed Leyland Titan double-deckers on all the Heswall routes before they were extended and these buses could not negotiate all the roads in the lower part of the village. So the Banks Road service became a separate local route, usually worked by a small bus, being allowed five minutes down the hill and nine minutes back.

Because these events coincided with the end of the augmented summer time tables, seasonal men were kept on to provide the extra staff needed and buses which would have been delicensed for the winter were kept running. The solid-tyred Leviathan double-deckers were no longer seen at New Ferry and they disappeared from West Kirby in 1931. They would have been quite unable to maintain the accelerated schedules.

Through Tickets & Contracts

There were a number of special clauses in the Agreement. Since 1928 Birkenhead Corporation had issued through bus and ferry return tickets to and from Liverpool on all routes and proposed to extend them to the new services. These tickets could be bought from conductors on the buses or at the ferry turnstiles and were available for return on day of issue or the following day. Later, Saturday's tickets were accepted for return on Mondays. It was agreed that Crosville would have the facility to issue and accept similar tickets over common sections of route and, to avoid practical difficulties, it was necessary to extend their availability to adjoining districts such as Pensby and Barnston. A Corporation ticket issued over a 'free trade' section could be used on a Crosville bus on the return journey or vice versa.

On the Parkgate buses, through tickets were available to and from Higher Bebington (Traveller's Rest). In the mid-'thirties, Crosville tried to extend the range of these tickets to Ellesmere Port and whilst the Corporation Transport department was willing, the Ferries department, who received only 2½d per ticket, would not agree. In 1938, the company managed to get further concessions, as will be seen later.

Crosville had issued a full range of monthly, 3, 6 and 12-monthly contracts between all points on the Heswall routes and Singleton Avenue or Woodside, no additional charge being made for the extended route on the contractors' buses. There had also been books of 12 prepaid tickets which were abolished. The Corporation, though not normally in favour of contracts, was commercially obliged to introduce them between Thurstaston, Irby and Woodside. Contracts from points within the protected area i.e. from Ivy Cottage inward were withdrawn and it was agreed that contracts from the common points, Heswall and Thingwall, would be issued only by Crosville but accepted also on Corporation buses. As the latter never did anything for nothing, it was arranged for the company to supply the Corporation with tickets which were issued to Crosville contractors riding on Corporation buses. Birkenhead was paid 5d for each Heswall ticket issued and 3¼d for each Thingwall ticket. Another provision of the Agreement gave Birkenhead Corporation the right to terminate in Heswall Bus Station for £5 per year.

The position of the local traffic restriction point on the Woodchurch Road routes depended upon the frequency of Corporation services but they so arranged matters that, from the outset, Crosville buses were prevented from carrying local passengers between Woodside and a point half way between Arrowe Park Gates and Thingwall Corner (known as Ivy Cottage) on the Heswall routes and Arrowe Brook Road corner (Arrowe House Farm) on the

Immediately before extension of the Heswall services to Woodside in 1930, Crosville placed Leyland Titan TD1 double-deckers in service at Heswall depot. Number 359 was one of a batch of 14 and had an unusual upper-deck emergency door which is visible on the offside. The oval logo was introduced during the LMS era being modified by eliminating LMS when the new company was formed in 1930. Note that the indicator box is empty. Renumbered L53 in 1935, it was fitted with a diesel engine after the 1939-45 War and ran until 1953.

West Kirby route. This gave the Corporation all the traffic between Birkenhead and Arrowe Park. The Corporation chose not to extend its buses beyond Lower Bebington to Clatterbridge at that time, so the Crosville New Ferry-Meols service with its short journeys to Spital Cross Roads continued to carry local traffic throughout.

The Corporation's powers to run to Greasby and Frankby were not exercised until April 1932 when a lengthy but infrequent route (85) was started between Woodside and Thurstaston via Park Station, Upton, Greasby, Frankby and Montgomery Hill. Crosville then withdrew one monthly journey between Park Station and Torpenhow Open Air School.

The impact of these greatly improved bus services on community life was gradual but dramatic, even though it took place at a time of economic depression and high unemployment. It took time for the facilities to become known so the increase in traffic on the New Chester Road services in the late summer of 1930 was limited but, by 1931, word had spread and trippers flocked across the ferry to crowd aboard the Crosville buses for Chester, North Wales, Parkgate and Heswall. There are unfortunately no detailed passenger figures available for comparison but Table 1 on page 39 sets out the changes in the number of timetabled journeys. The elimination of the tiresome change of vehicle on the outskirts of Birkenhead encouraged travel and the residential development of Wirral was stimulated enormously. The new routes hit the railway companies hard though, by virtue of their substantial shareholding in Crosville, they had hedged their bets. Although the bus journey was slower than by train, many Birkenhead-Chester passengers chose Crosville as the bus terminus in the Market Square, across the road from the Cathedral, was so much more convenient for the city centre than the General Railway Station.

There is no doubt that the Birkenhead shopkeepers and cinema proprietors benefited enormously from the through buses as journeys which had been tedious became swift, easy and, in many cases, cheaper. The main services were so frequent that trips could be made on impulse.

Fares

In the very early days of Crosville's rural services, fares were fixed for the principal stages and the conductors were expected to use their judgement in charging pro rata for intermediate journeys, doubtless the cause of much argument with passengers. As the network developed, fares were fixed more formally at about 1½d per mile (minimum 2d) and return tickets were offered at reduced rates. Between New Ferry and Eastham cheap single fares were available before 8.30-9.0am and after 5.0pm on Mondays to Fridays at a halfpenny or a penny less than the ordinary fare while at Hoylake there was a most generous local concession, giving return travel at single fare, not only before 9.0am but

Port Sunlight, with its Soap Works, model village and Lady Lever Art Gallery, was a popular venue for private party outings between the wars. This impressive convoy is led by AEC Regal T5 (formerly 980) which came with the business of Wirral Motor Transport whose Birkenhead-Bangor service was taken over in February 1934.

In 1929, a new series of Leyland Lions was launched and No. 341, an LT1, was one of the first. It is seen in an alternative, rather dull all-maroon livery applied to some vehicles in the early 'thirties. Note the early design of Leyland body with rather square rear end, contrasting with the more curved lines of Leyland bodies on later Lions and Tigers. The front wheels are of the same type as used on the earlier PLSC Lions. This bus became C19 in 1935 but all 25 LT1s were withdrawn and sold in 1936.

The Leyland Titan TD2 had a more powerful engine, was one foot longer and embodied various technical improvements over the TD1. No.645 was exhibited at the Commercial Motor Show in 1931. Four more of the same batch, (646-9) entered service in 1932 and 649 (later M1) was the first diesel-engined double-decker in the Crosville fleet. The TD2 was the last model to have the short radiator, a type with straighter sides than the earlier TD1s. This bus became L68 and then M22 when fitted with a diesel engine in 1938. Most of this type were rebodied with standard Tilling-style Eastern Coach Works bodies and lasted until late in the fifties.

also between 12.0noon and 2.0pm on weekdays.

One penny (d) stages were adopted on most routes in the Spring of 1928 but return fares were increased. When the Road Traffic Act 1930 took effect, the fares in force on 9th February 1931 were frozen and could be altered only by application to the Traffic Commissioners who required proof of financial need.

The general effect of the 1930 developments on fares favoured the passenger. Many single fares were reduced as demonstrated in Table 2 ,only contract rates tending to move slightly upwards. On the Heswall and Parkgate routes from Woodside, Crosville adopted Corporation workmen's return conditions throughout the route; these were more generous than their own. Monthly contracts were available on the West Kirby-Park Station and Liscard routes with half rate for school children and apprentices; grammar school pupils could travel more cheaply – and faster – between Moreton and Wallasey schools than they could on the municipal buses which had no contract facilities. There were also cheap school singles and returns within Ellesmere Port. A few anomalies were created by the new restrictions on carriage of local passengers but these affected only infrequent services. Thus one could travel from New Ferry to Lower Bebington on a Meols bus but not on one bound for Raby Mere; along Woodchurch Road a New Ferry-Moreton Shore bus could carry local passengers between the Half Way House and Arrowe Park but the more frequent Heswall buses were barred. Eventually local passengers did not attempt to stop Crosville buses so the exceptions to the restrictions were of little value to the company.

In 1935 the Commissioners initiated talks with a view to standardising fares charged by the three Wirral operators – Birkenhead and Wallasey Corporations and Crosville and this resulted in many fares being reduced in 1936 when Crosville adopted municipal conditions for workmen's and children's fares in and adjoining the municipal operating areas. This gave free travel for children under five (instead of three) and workmen's returns at single fare in most cases. Fares then remained unchanged until 1951! On certain sections, Crosville fares had been influenced by cheap railway fares and Birkenhead-Chester for 1/6 ($7\frac{1}{2}$p) single and 2/- (10p) return was a bargain in 1930 not to mention 1951. Through 1/3d return tickets between West Kirby, Hoylake, Meols and Liverpool via Park Station and the Mersey Railway, introduced on Saturday afternoons and Sundays in the summer of 1932, were short-lived

The Last Pre-war Days

Once the basic network had been established, the Crosville route map changed very little. Traffic continued to expand as economic conditions improved gradually throughout the decade. Some of the increase was absorbed by substituting double-deck buses for single-deckers. At the time of the 1930 Agreement, Crosville owned very few double-deck buses. There were the 12 obsolescent Leyland Leviathans

Because of bodywork deterioration,. said to have been caused by washing by high-pressure hoses, most of both the A (PLSC1) and B (PLSC3) classes were rebodied stylishly by Eastern Coach Works during the mid-'thirties, the overall effect being marred by retention of the original radiator. Nevertheless, as shown here, they were considered good enough for local private hires. Number B35 (formerly 74) was one of the last of its type to enter service and remained on the road until 1950.

with their solid tyres and wooden seats and a few open toppers of the same model acquired with the business of White Rose of Rhyl. From 1930 Leyland Titans were purchased in increasing numbers and these low height vehicles, so eminently suitable for rural work, gradually spread on to the Ellesmere Port and Chester routes. However, Crosville remained essentially a single-deck company, the double-deckers being concentrated in Liverpool, Wirral, Chester and Crewe with a few along the North Wales coast. The Mold, Loggerheads and Holywell services saw no double-deck operation in pre-war days.

The opening of Crosville's Rock Ferry depot on 1st April 1932 eased accommodation and bus maintenance problems. Sixty-eight vehicles were based there from the opening day, the Woodside-Parkgate buses being transferred from Heswall and the coaches from West Kirby.

At summer weekends the demand from holidaymakers and day trippers was enormous and traffic increased every year. The industrial and residential expansion of Ellesmere Port was another growing source of revenue. Workmen's day return tickets at 10d were available from both Birkenhead and Chester and special buses ran to the expanding oil installations at Stanlow and Bowaters' Paper Mill. Most of the internal needs of Ellesmere Port were provided by the through services but the local services between Great Sutton, Rivacre, Whitby and the Port which were eventually needed were expensive to operate as they had to be run from Chester or Birkenhead depots.

An addition to the network was the Wrexham-Birkenhead express, acquired with the business of the Western Transport Co. Ltd. on 1st May 1933. It ran on Mondays to Fridays only and had only one fare – 2/6d single or return. Its terminus was in Church Street, just above Woodside where the ex-Western Transport Tilling Stevens bus which invariably operated it stood from its arrival at 11.15am until its 8.30pm departure.

Tunnel Bus Schemes

The first Mersey road tunnel, Queensway, between Liverpool and Birkenhead was opened on 18th July 1934 and, early in August, Crosville applied to extend the Loggerheads/Pantymwyn-Mold-Woodside services through to Liverpool. The City Police were prepared to allocate stands in Hotham Street, a side street off London Road and, to comply with protection for the Mersey Railway provided for in the Mersey Tunnel Acts, the company proposed to adopt Ledsham Station as the first setting down point from Liverpool and vice versa. At a three-day hearing before the Traffic Commissioners, the application was bitterly opposed by Liverpool and Birkenhead Corporations and the Mersey Tunnel Joint Committee on the grounds that tunnel bus services, of which they purported to approve, should be planned on a regional basis so the Commissioners reserved their decision for six months to give the objectors time to draw up their plans. The Mold applications were refused as were the subsequent appeals to the Minister but in March 1936, Crosville and Ribble jointly applied for an hourly service between Southport and Chester to be formed by linking part of the Southport-Liverpool and Woodside-Ellesmere Port-Chester services. There was to be protection for local operators and the railways between Seaforth and Overpool Cemetery Gates.

In the subsequent proceedings, the opposing local authorities were represented by eminent Counsel, both destined to hold Cabinet rank – David Maxwell-Fyfe (later Lord Kilmuir) and Hartley Shawcross (later Lord Shawcross). This application was no more successful than the earlier one and a policy for tunnel bus services had still not been worked out when the war broke out in 1939. Only long distance coach services were permitted to use it.

A New Agreement

The 1930 Agreement was valid for seven years and then terminable by six months' notice. In general, it had been a great success but the spread of housing estates in the Wirral villages and a few operational problems made it desirable to make some adjustments.

The Corporation's service from Woodside to Thurstaston via Park Station, Greasby and Frankby ran only every 90 minutes and attracted very little traffic so the operators agreed that Greasby and Frankby should be served exclusively by Crosville from Park Station and exclusively by the Corporation from Woodside. They also agreed that, if it so wished, the Corporation could link its two Thurstaston services as a circular via Greasby and via Irby, but would relinquish its unexercised right to run via Irby Mill Hill. The Corporation and Crosville would share the traffic on the Upton to Saughall Massie road and, if a service ever became necessary, on Wood Lane, Greasby.

The Corporation could extend its Woodside-Pool Lane short working of the Eastham service to Raeburn Avenue, Bromborough but without prejudice to the company's right to run along Allport Lane if that road should be extended to Eastham in the future. Finally, the Corporation could extend its Woodside-Spital Cross Roads service to Brimstage Cross Roads and back along Mount Road to Birkenhead as a circular but, if it did so, it must give protection to Crosville and not pick up passengers between Brimstage Cross Roads and Marsh Lane.

There was some argument about through bus and ferry tickets which had never been available from Frankby or Greasby. Under the new arrangements the Corporation proposed to run buses from Woodside to Greasby via Arrowe Park and Arrowe Brook Road, a route followed by Crosville's Woodside-Meols service as far as Arrowe Bridge. The same service also served the Farmers' Arms at Frankby and Lower Caldy Cross Roads, which were also on the Woodside-Thurstaston via Greasby route. The company thought that the proposed bus and ferry tickets from Frankby and Greasby were too low and would compete unfairly with their Liverpool traffic transferring to the Mersey Railway at Park Station. However, the fares complied with the Corporation's rigid formula and it would have been difficult to raise them without creating anomalies with other routes. Eventually, Crosville withdrew their objection in return for similar facilities right through to West Kirby though whether these had much value in practice is open to debate.

A supplementary Agreement was signed on 22nd April 1938 and remained in force with only one serious dispute until 1972 when a new Agreement was made with the PTE.

Frequent Corporation buses along Allport Lane and Allport Road, Bromborough sealed the fate of the infrequent summer service between Rock Ferry Pier and Raby Mere. The Corporation declined to take over, Clarke remarking that there was insufficient traffic for a taxi and it ran for the last time on 3rd September 1938; from the following day the Heswall via Storeton service was diverted from Rock Ferry Pier to Woodside via Thornton Road and Borough Road. The ferry itself closed less than a year later.

In 1938, there was a meeting, convened at Crosville's request, with Wallasey Corporation though no record of the proceedings has been found. Probably the company sought an extension from Liscard to New Brighton but, no doubt, the Corporation was as obdurate as ever. The electrification of the Wirral lines in March 1938 resulted in considerable loss of bus traffic on parallel bus routes.

With war clouds gathering, Crosville could look back with pride on the achievements of the 'thirties. The doubts of 1930 had been dispelled and, whilst there was always some regret and resentment at the price paid to get the buses down to Woodside, the gains had justified the sacrifice. The late C.R. Buckley, a Crosville trainee who later held high rank within the National Bus Company, described it as the best thing that ever happened to the company. Meticulous observance of the Agreement by both sides had developed mutual trust between them and enabled both to expand their traffic without dissipating their resources in wasteful competition and legal expenses.

The company had expanded its services in North Wales but unfortunately there are no separate statistics for the Wirral districts. Suffice it to say that 402 vehicles had carried 37.9 million passengers in 1930 over the whole system and in 1938-39, 995 vehicles carried 94.5 million passengers. The 30-odd double-deckers in 1930 had become 150.

TABLE 1
NO.OF SCHEDULED JOURNEYS OPERATED BEFORE AND AFTER EXTENSION TO WOODSIDE 1930

(Excluding Duplicates and Special Trips)

Route	No.of Outward Journeys Operated on Mondays to Fridays		
	May 1928	October 1930	July 1931
Chester Direct	9	16	28
Chester via Ellesmere Port	22	31	35
Ellesmere Port via Pooltown Road	—	23	15
Heswall via Pensby	41	51	57
Heswall via Barnston	21	39	39
Parkgate	11	22	29
West Kirby via Irby Mill Hill	4	7	12
TOTAL	108	189	215

TABLE 2
COMPARISON OF FARES BEFORE & AFTER EXTENSION OF CROSVILLE SERVICES TO WOODSIDE 1930

TO/FROM WOODSIDE &	FARES 1928-30*			1930-36			1936-51			1930-51
	S	R	Pre-paid	S	WR	R	S	WR	R	Bus & Ferry
Chester	1/9½	2/9	-	1/6	-	2/-	1/6	-	2/-	-
Ellesmere Port	1/0½	-	-	10d	1/2	1/5	10d	10d	1/4	-
Great Sutton	11½d	-	-	9d	-	-	9d	-	1/4	-
Little Sutton	10½d			8d		1/2	8d		1/2	
Eastham	7½d	1/-	-	6d	6d	-	5d	5d	-	1/-
Loggerheads	2/9½	4/5	-	2/7	-	4/-	2/7	-	4/-	-
Mold	2/3½	3/7	-	2/2	-	3/3	2/2	-	3/3	-
Queensferry	1/5½	2/7	-	1/4	-	2/6	1/4	-	2/6	-
Parkgate	1/-	1/8	-	1/-	1/-	1/6	1/-	1/-	1/4	-
Neston	11d	1/7	-	11d	11d	1/5	11d	11d	1/3	-
Thornton Hough	8d	1/2	-	8d	8d	1/-	8d	8d	11d	-
Clatterbridge	6d	-	-	6d	6d	9d	6d	6d	8d	-
Hr.Bebington	4d	7d	-	4d	4d	6d	3d	3d	-	6d
Heswall	10d	1/-§	8d	7d	7d	-	7d	7d	-	1/4
Thurstaston	9d	11d§	7d	6d	6d	-	6d	6d	-	1/2
Pensby, Irby or Barnston	9d	11d§	7d	6d	6d	-	5d	5d	-	1/2
Ivy Cottage	6d	10d§	6d	5d	5d	-	4d	4d	-	1/-
West Kirby	1/-	-	-	11d	-	1/4	9d	-	1/2	1/4#
Caldy	10d	-	-	9d	-	1/2	7d	-	1/-	1/2#
Frankby	8d	-	-	7d	-	-	6d	-	10d	1/-#
Irby Mill Hill	7d	-	-	6d	-	-	6d	6d	10d	1/-#
Arrowe House Farm	6d	-	-	4d	-	-	4d	4d	-	10d

* including tram fares. § Workmen's return available up to about 8.15am plus tram fares. # introduced 2.7.39
S -Single R - Ordinary Return WR - Workmen's Return

Crosville's original route, the Chester-Ellesmere Port-Birkenhead service, carried considerable local traffic as Ellesmere Port and the surrounding villages were built up and double-deck buses were regularly used. Leyland Titan TD1 L3, a 1931 bus originally numbered 20 is seen on the stand in Chester Market Square in late 'thirties livery. After being fitted with a diesel engine it was renumbered M199 and ran until 1953.

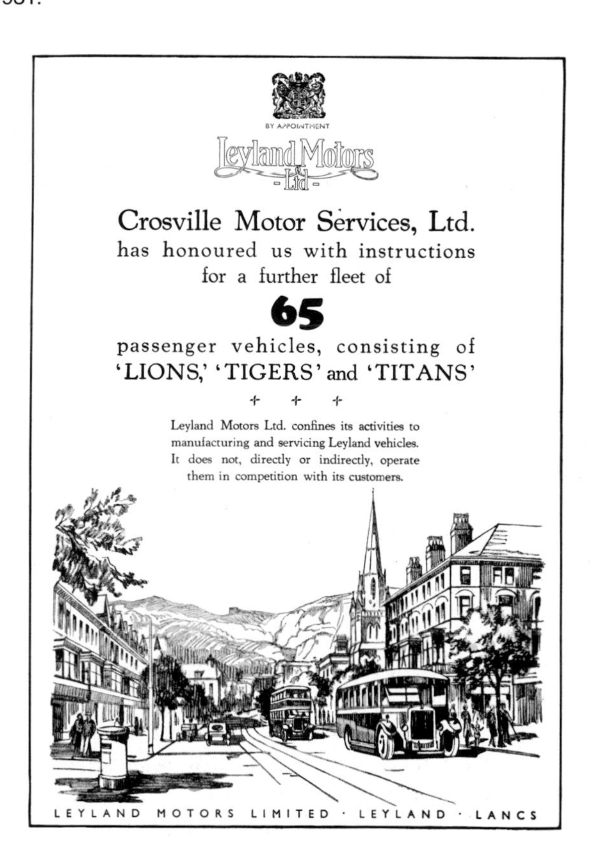

Reproduced from Tramway and Railway World, 17th September 1931.

CHAPTER 5

THE WAR, 1939-45

The outbreak of war on 3rd September 1939 cut short a busy summer season. The Chairman of the Traffic Commissioners assumed dictatorial powers as the Regional Transport Commissioner and the immediate priorities were the conservation of fuel and rubber supplies all of which, in those days, had to be imported. Some preliminary planning had already been done and operators had been warned to prepare schedules with 40% cuts. Other priorities were connected with the blackout which, initially, was almost total making driving at night extremely hazardous.

Some cuts were implemented immediately as passenger demand, particularly in the evenings, fell dramatically but from 24th September, the formal cuts came into force. The following services were totally withdrawn:-

Birkenhead (Woodside)-Holywell
Birkenhead (Woodside)-Heswall via Storeton
New Ferry-Moreton Shore
Liscard-Heswall/Parkgate
Wrexham-Birkenhead (Woodside)
Wavertree (Clock Tower)-Warrington via Cronton
Birkenhead (Woodside)-Loggerheads/Pantymwyn curtailed at Mold
Birkenhead (Park Stn)-West Kirby via Saughall Massie curtailed at Overchurch Road.

Frequencies on other routes were radically reduced and late buses cancelled.

However, much of Crosville territory was considered 'safe' from enemy bombing and there was a move not only to establish new war industries but to evacuate others from danger areas. Plans were also made to extend other strategic industries such as the Ellesmere Port oil installations. On Merseyside there was a ready supply of labour and demands soon arose for new services to factories around Chester and Deeside. A typical example was Vickers Armstrong's aircraft works at Broughton, near Queensferry which was served fromWoodside in 1940; some trips eventually ran through to and from Liverpool via the Mersey Tunnel. Stanlow was served as far as possible by rail, a new station being opened in December 1940, but Crosville had to provide a service starting from Bromborough Pool Lane, to serve the workers living too far from a railway station.

After the first few months of the 'phoney war' there were some relaxations and in 1940 fuel was made available for some summer duplication. However, aerial attacks which started in August 1940 caused a migration of people from the towns to the Wirral villages; they overcrowded the already severely strained Crosville services and created serious problems for the company. Rock Ferry and Liverpool

In 1942 the Ministry of Supply 'unfroze' a number of Leyland TD7 chassis, had them fitted with utility bodywork and issued them to operators. After the war, they were fitted with Tilling-style indicators at the front and upgraded in different ways. M128 (FFM 178) with a Brush body has been repainted with three cream bands and fitted with sliding ventilators on both decks while M132 with Willowbrook bodywork still has only a single opening window on each side of each deck, which was the wartime specification. Both buses were withdrawn in 1956.

A post-war view of Bristol K6A MB173, delivered in 1945 (as M173) with Strachan body to Ministry of Supply wartime specification with slatted wooden seats and only two opening windows on each side which were later added to. Note the high radiator, typical of pre-war and wartime Bristols. There were 22 vehicles in the batch and they were the first to be painted Tilling green from new.

Although the oval logo dates this view as some time before the outbreak of war, the Territorial Army passengers exemplify the spirit of the times. Of the later Lions, the LT3 Model (the E class from 1935) was the most numerous. No. E63 was one of 25 placed in service in 1932 and kept running until 1950.

depots narrowly escaped serious damage in the air raids which reached a climax in an eight-night attack from 1st to 8th May 1941. Liverpool city centre was devastated and, for some time, buses could not reach the Pier Head. There was a temporary terminus at the foot of Mount Pleasant, an involuntary reversion to the pre-1932 arrangements.

In Liverpool, the Lockheed aircraft factory at Speke engaged staff from Widnes and coal miners were recruited in Liverpool for Cronton Colliery, a dedicated service being provided. Following the fall of France, the general increase in port activity on both sides of the river created full employment, a situation unknown on Merseyside for decades. The transport demand was insatiable and was handled only because there was considerable shift work, allowing the load to be spread.

Companies such as Crosville suffered from worse staff problems than the municipal operators as the working conditions were less favourable. The Regional Transport Commissioner arranged for Birkenhead and Wallasey Corporations to run some special shift services to Ellesmere Port and Chester as Crosville simply did not have the resources. In March 1944, Crosville asked Birkenhead to extend some trips on its Lower Bebington service (50) to Clatterbridge Hospital to ease its problems.

Despite the government's 'Is your journey really necessary?' campaign, the public, weighed down by wartime problems, took occasional outings to Parkgate, Chester, West Kirby or North Wales and, on fine summer Sundays, the buses were crammed to capacity. For this reason, Sunday facilities were severely restricted from 1943, not only to save the fuel but to give the overworked staff a rest.

The public, of course, did not understand the operational problems and there was dissatisfaction that Crosville buses were prohibited from carrying local traffic in Birkenhead even under wartime conditions. At a series of meetings in 1941, the company pointed out that at peak hours there were no vacant seats anyway, this being demonstrated by a request to Birkenhead to issue contracts from Thingwall on the same terms as Crosville as the company's ticket holders were travelling on Corporation buses and creating extra clerical work! From 1st July 1942, Crosville Thingwall contracts ceased to be available on Corporation buses. After a conference in December 1941, the Birkenhead Council passed a resolution deploring the 'trivial nature of

There were 54 of these Eastern Coach Works bodied Leyland Titan TD5s (M47-100) delivered between 1938 and 1940, this being the last big Leyland double-deck order and the last delivery of pre-war models. These buses were fitted with destination blinds from new.

the modification (of the existing rules) offered by the company'. But the company knew that more stops meant extra running time, more buses and staff and the Regional Transport Commissioner upheld their stand.

The worse affected area was Eastham as, to save fuel, the Corporation service had been curtailed at Allport Road, except for a few peak hour trips and passengers had to rely on Crosville buses coming through from Chester, Ellesmere Port and North Wales. They were often full but the Commissioner refused to allocate any extra fuel and eventually the Corporation found the fuel to run extra Eastham trips by cancelling journeys on other services.

One wartime phenomenon which the company was spared on Merseyside was the large military camp. A small RAF station was built in West Kirby Road, Saughall Massie, which was not on a regular bus route; there were evening and weekend services to and from West Kirby via Black Horse Hill and occasional specials to and from Meols station via Heron Road. These continued for some years after the war.

Wartime Economics

The need to eliminate all unnecessary journeys created ideal conditions for reducing mileage to a minimum and increasing seat-occupancy to the maximum. Costs increased very considerably and profits fell but so many more passengers were carried that no fare increases could be justified. The following table shows the extent to which traffic increased with a very reduced mileage. The indexing (1939 = 100) shows, for example, that in 1945, when the buses ran 14% less mileage than in 1939, productivity in terms of revenue per mile was 2.19 times greater. The data is for Crosville as a whole.

Year Ending 31st March	Revenue £000s	Index	Passengers 000s	Index	Mileage 000s	Index	Pence (d) per bus mile.	Index
1939	1,250	100	94,455	100	33,465	100	8.98	100
1940	1,395	116	100,527	106	30,419	91	11.00	122
1941	1,741	139	115,900	123	28,348	85	14.74	164
1942	2,084	167	134,549	142	29,807	89	16.78	187
1943	2,044	164	129,836	137	26,738	80	18.34	204
1944	2,263	181	141,346	150	28,000	84	19.40	216
1945	2,366	189	148,544	157	28,859	86	19.68	219
1946	2,353	188	149,420	158	30,161	90	18.75	209

CHAPTER 6
POST-WAR WIRRAL

The end of the war in 1945 unleashed a pent-up demand for leisure travel which no operator was able to satisfy fully. Petrol and diesel fuel was still rationed and new buses were in short supply. Many of the buses still in service would have been scrapped years earlier if pre-war policies had prevailed. Passengers carried on the whole network increased from 94.5 million in 1938-39 to 158.5 million in 1946-47, a rise of 68% for a fleet expansion of 16%. No separate figures for Wirral are available though it is known that, between 1946 and 1952, the Chester-Ellesmere Port-Birkenhead group of services alone accounted for 11% of the company's revenue. Fine Sundays and Bank Holidays would see up to 60 double-deck buses, mostly from Rock Ferry, but assisted by Chester and Heswall, running up to 200 duplicate trips from Woodside. Much last minute planning went into organising the return movement of this traffic and mobile patrols were used to divert buses as necessary. In 1948, 175.7 million passengers were carried followed by a peak of 193 million in both 1949 and 1950. Carryings then remained around the 180 million mark until 1956 after which there was a gradual decline.

Some suspended facilities were restored in 1946 including the Heswall via Storeton and Chester-Meols direct services, the latter being diverted via Willaston. Frequencies were increased and routes such as Loggerheads, Pantymwyn, Holywell and Chester-Meols were double-decked; Birkenhead-Chester direct had a 15-minute service for the 1947 season with part double and part single-deck buses. The constant shortage of buses resulted in no new services being introduced until 1950 by which time the post-war demand was beginning to tail off. An hourly Liscard-Parkgate summer service was started, Birkenhead Corporation having agreed to free trade between Moreton, Upton and Arrowe Park on the understanding that the pre-war New Ferry-Moreton Shore service should not be reintroduced. The following year, when a Liscard-Chester service (C26, later F49) was added, they were not so magnanimous, resulting in two services with different passenger restrictions covering the same section of route. This was relaxed when frequencies were reduced.

In 1950-51, the intensity of bus usage, measured in terms of average passengers carried per mile run was 30% higher than in 1938-39; ten years later it was still 9% higher but social changes had created peaks and troughs in demand which made averages less typical. The five day week was a mixed blessing as it robbed the operators of considerable commuting revenue and left them with an obligation to maintain under-used peak hour services for the residual Saturday workers. On the other hand, for companies like Crosville, it released vehicles in the summer for use on profitable express services and private hire work. This led to the allocation of dual-purpose vehicles to the Wirral depots. However, the advent of television tore a great hole in evening and Saturday afternoon traffic but the duty to keep buses hanging around for three or four hours to work last journeys remained.

The gradual dispersal of the population both residentially and to new outlying work places, added to the peak hour demand. More and more vehicles were able to make only one trip per peak period leading to the need to increase the fleet at a time of falling traffic. Demands for school transport, at concessionary fares, and the shortening of the working day to the extent that school and worker demands sometimes overlapped exacerbated these problems. However, it was the growth of private transport that had the greatest effect on bus patronage and it worsened every year. Crosville in Wirral was particularly hard hit as many districts in its operating area had above average car ownership. The MALTS Survey of 1966 showed that the figure for Wirral was 44% higher than on Merseyside east of the Mersey but, as Birkenhead's figure was equal to the average for Merseyside as a whole, all the other areas, Hoylake, Heswall etc. had the highest car ownership rates in the region. Furthermore, traffic loss was greater in the off-peak periods than at the peak. An analysis of trips to and from Liverpool city centre showed that about 22% of work trips were by private transport but the rate for social and recreational trips was 34%.

Urbanisation of the Wirral villages brought demands for new local services. West Kirby to Greenbank Road and Fulton Avenue, (both via Black Horse Hill as Greenbank Road did not go through until 1957) started in 1950 and Heswall to Somerset Road, (the latter shared with Birkenhead Corporation), followed in 1951. The year 1954 saw some journeys on New Ferry-West Kirby re-routed through Raby Village and the Woodside-Burton route diverted through Little Neston. Road improvements enabled most of the Somerset Road journeys to be absorbed in the further diversion of New Ferry-West Kirby buses via Irby Road and Irby village. From 1964 some journeys ran from Irby via Irby Mill Hill and Montgomery Hill, using a road which had never before had a bus service. A Hoylake-Greasby via Pump Lane service was started in 1956 under pressure from Hoylake UDC; it survived some changes including an extension to Cortsway but was totally abandoned in 1958.

Ellesmere Port

Other new facilities were Woodside-Ellesmere Port-Helsby-Frodsham (1952) and Ellesmere Port-Hooton-Willaston-

Bristol K5G MB163 was a mixture having originated with London Transport as B4 in May 1942 and was purchased by Crosville together with 13 others at the end of 1952. On arrival, some of the worn out utility bodies were removed and replaced by others, MB163 receiving the 1945 Strachan body from MB184. To lengthen its life further, in 1956 the 1949 Eastern Coach Works body from M248 was fitted, the whole ensemble then running until 1959. When photographed at Woodside, the bus was based at Flint depot and running on the Holywell service. Whilst the destination display is descriptive of the route, the service number is wrong, the correct one being 130 according to the Rock Ferry blinds or 135 if you believed the timetable!

Leyland TD1 M576 was originally Bury Corporation No. 20 and was purchased in 1946 as L102. The original petrol engine was replaced by a Leyland diesel in May 1948 following which the vehicle was renumbered. It retained its original 1930 Massey body to which the standard Tilling indicators were added. It is seen at Rock Ferry depot prior to departure on a works journey to the oil installations at Thornton-le-Moors. It was scrapped in 1953.

Among the relatively younger second-hand buses purchased in the post-war years were three 1936 Leyland TD4c models from Chesterfield Corporation of which No. M516 was numerically the first. They had Metro-Cammell all-metal bodies and required little attention, Tilling indicators and sliding windows being fitted. Torque-convertors were replaced by crash gearboxes before entering Crosville service. The scene is Heswall depot yard. After withdrawal in 1955, M516 served at least two further years with Sir Alfred McAlpine and Son Ltd., contractors.

A dignified bus against a noble red sandstone backcloth in Hoylake in February 1953. The bus is MW379, a 1949 Bristol K6B with 55-seat lowbridge Eastern Coach Works body, new in 1949. This was the typical new Crosville double-deck bus of the post-war period and is in original condition except for the absence of the cream upper deck window pillars. The Chester-Meols service had been converted to double-deck operation in the post-war period because of the much heavier demand.

Neston-Parkgate-Heswall-West Kirby (1957), which started as a summer holiday service but works and school trips were later added. Ellesmere Port had had a few local services before the war. On Wednesdays, Saturdays and Sundays in the summer a bus had come out from Chester and worked three routes to Rivacre Valley Swimming Pool from Whitby (Sportsman's Arms) via Merseyton Road or via Pooltown Road and from Childer Thornton via Little Sutton and on Fridays and Saturdays there were trips between the Grosvenor Hotel and Great Sutton or Rivacre via Grange Farm Estate and Overpool. All these were suspended during the war and never resumed in the same form and it was not until 1954 that a small local network was started to serve new estates in Great Sutton. At first, the facilities were a little ahead of the demand and in 1956, it was found more economical to serve some districts by diverting through buses. In the 'sixties, Ellesmere Port expanded rapidly, new roads altering the geography of the town. In 1963, there was a general revision of the Chester-Ellesmere Port-Birkenhead routes to serve some new estates and the local network was revived with routes to Great Sutton, Wolverham, Overpool and Rivacre. A second change was necessary three months later, to rectify inadequacies. A small bus station had been opened at Marina Parade on 9th September 1962 but the absence of a depot in the town made local operation costly. This was not put right until 1972 when about 12 buses were based at the bus station, as a sub-depot of Rock Ferry. A new bus station was opened on an adjoining site in April 1974 whereafter control of Ellesmere Port changed to Chester depot to fit in with new local authority boundaries. The network of local services was considerably expanded.

Special Works Services

During the war, numerous dedicated works services were provided to enable often remotely located factories to recruit labour over a wide area and this trend continued and expanded in the post-war years. Many of these services were subsidised by employers and restricted to the employees of a particular plant. Work started on the Atomic Energy factory beside the railway line at Capenhurst on 24th August 1949; this was Europe's first plant for the production of enriched uranium and was still the only one in Britain 40 years later. The UKAEA obtained a road service licence for a service between the factory and Little Sutton, for emergency use and the railway served Birkenhead and Chester. In 1952 when full production had been reached, Crosville was providing a comprehensive network of shift services covering Chester, Deeside and the whole of Wirral including places not normally served such as New Brighton, Seacombe and suburban Birkenhead. The Authority put workers from various districts on the same shift so that most routes operated only on particular shifts. The car ownership explosion caused an enormous extension to the oil refineries at Stanlow and special services from Birkenhead, Chester, Neston, Heswall and Moreton were needed. Two bus stations were built at Stanlow North and Thornton Underpass. From the end of 1962 there was the Vauxhall works at Ellesmere Port with new services from Woodside (F3) and Chester (C5). Trips on the former were extended to and from Liverpool for a time but soon withdrawn due to poor patronage. A Chester journey was altered to start from Wrexham in October 1963 and this eventually became a separate service from Rhos (G67).

The era of long workpeople's services was a short and generally profitless one for most operators who often agreed to run them to prevent independent coach operators getting a foot in the door. Typical was F57, originally from Upton, but soon extended from West Kirby, to Runcorn ICI Offices which ran from 1962 to 1966. The worker was soon likely to tire of a 1 hr journey morning and evening and a weekly fare of £2-6-8d (£2.33) and either acquire private transport or seek employment nearer home. Special buses to the Broughton aircraft factory (F13) continued to operate

A post-war view of 1938 Leyland Titan TD5 M67 rebuilt with Tilling indicators and seen at Heswall Bus Station on 17th February 1951. Note the painted radiator shell. This bus achieved the company's (quite normal at the time) 21-year life span.

One of the first Eastern Coach Works bodied Bristol L6As, No. KB24 (Later SLA24), seen at Banks Road terminus, Lower Heswall, was originally a 35-seat rear-entrance bus when delivered in June 1947. Twenty-seven of these buses were rebuilt for one-man operation in 1957 with forward-entrance and electrically-operated jack-knife doors controlled by the driver. The front bulkhead was partially angled to facilitate fare collection. It was sold to a contractor in 1965 and finally broken up five years later.

Leyland Tiger TS7 KA21 with Harrington bus body was new in 1937, the cutaway canopy setting a new modern standard for Crosville's single-deck fleet. In 1950, 27 of these buses were rebuilt by the company with new panelling, sliding ventilators and cream window surrounds. The bus is seen in Thornton Hough village on 9th July 1959.

Bristol KSW6B DKB434 was already nine years old when observed leaving Woodside in April 1961 on a works service to Bowaters' Paper Mill, Ellesmere Port. It was originally numbered MW434 and the unusual positions of the fleet number plates are noteworthy. These were the first post-war highbridge buses to operate in Wirral and were particularly useful in places like Ellesmere Port where there was a high proportion of short-distance traffic. This bus was one of five sold to Yates' Tours of Runcorn in 1968 and it was scrapped the following year.

Although equipped for one-man operation, Bristol MW6G SMG372, was conductor-operated when operating this busy trip on the Woodside-Meols via Irby Mill Hill and Caldy service when new in September 1959. The scene is Woodchurch Road, Birkenhead near the Woodchurch Estate.

until the 'seventies and there was also a service from Woodside to Shotton Steel Works (F14) until 1969.

Relations with the Municipalities

Generally, the Agreements with Wallasey and Birkenhead Corporations stood the test of time very well. Crosville was in conflict with Wallasey twice, the first occasion being in 1953 when Wallasey wanted to serve its new cemetery which was well outside the borough boundary at Frankby. Crosville submitted its own application and opposed Wallasey on the grounds that it had run a service from Liscard to Heswall via Frankby in pre-war days. However this had not been reintroduced and the Corporation's licence was granted with a restriction that buses should not stop to pick up or set down passengers between Moreton Cross and Frankby.

In 1966 there was another dispute when Crosville proposed to run a new service from Liscard to Clatterbridge Hospital via Woodside for visitors. This was opposed by both municipal operators on the grounds that the existing services were adequate and their view was upheld by the Traffic Commissioners.

The only serious dispute with Birkenhead Corporation was in 1960 when the question of serving Mill Park Estate, Eastham arose. Birkenhead had been running a few buses for building workers since 1954 but the population now justified an all-day service. They proposed to extend their existing Woodside-Eastham village service to Mill Park and their Woodside-Bromborough (Raeburn Avenue) service via Heygarth Road to Eastham village. Crosville held that Mill Park was strictly speaking beyond Eastham village and therefore in their area and also that, had Allport Lane then been extended (which it later was, as Bridle Road) they would be entitled to use it. Birkenhead reminded the company that the 1930 Agreement forbade them running a service originating in Bebington and ending in Birkenhead. No agreement could be reached so both operators applied for and were granted licences, the new services being brought in together on 17th October 1960. The Crosville service (F7) ran hourly with a journey time of 28 minutes while the Corporation ran every 24 minutes with a 31-minute journey time so there were times when two buses ran together. The company buses could not pick up after leaving Allport Road so their catchment area was very restricted. Nevertheless, this arrangement persisted for over 13 years.

Bebington Corporation never tired of trying to get picking up restrictions lifted on Crosville buses. On 2nd April 1968 there was a joint census on New Chester Road after which both operators agreed that no change was desirable but after another count at the top of Thornton Road it was agreed that Crosville buses could pick up on Thornton Road at Heswall Avenue.

Declining Traffic

The national company bus strike, timed to hit the peak of the holiday season in July 1957 caused a serious loss of traffic, most of which was never regained. Passengers carried declined by 7.5% in that year. Frequencies were now being reduced and economy measures actively sought. From 1st November 1959, the circular workings between Park Station and West Kirby, which had originated in 1924, were replaced by Liscard-West Kirby-Frankby-Park Station and Newton-Greenbank Road-West Kirby-Moreton-Park Station services, with additional workings at peak hours. The new linking was dictated by economical timetabling as the new workings had no value as through routes; it was to last for almost 20 years. In 1966, service frequencies were

Bristol L6A No. KB6, new in 1946, originally carried a similar Eastern Coach Works 35-seat bus body which was replaced by a 1949 32-seat dual-purpose body removed from KA191 in January 1958. Renumbered ELA6 in 1958, it ran in this condition until 1961 after which it saw a further eight years' service with Atomic Power Constructions Ltd.

still comparable with those of 1959 though much summer augmentation had gone or had been reduced to the period of the school holidays. The biggest reductions were on the longer day tripper services such as Woodside-Denbigh, halved from four daily trips to two and Loggerheads from 30-60 minutes to two-hourly, augmented in school holidays. But Woodside-Heswall via Pensby still justified a 10-minute frequency on Saturday afternoons. The most affluent areas showed the greatest reductions – Liscard-West Kirby from 20 to 40 minutes and the Meols-Caldy local was withdrawn altogether in September 1965.

Towards the end of the sixties, there was an attempt to counteract falling traffic by running faster services. The Woodside-Holywell service (F8) became limited stop between Woodside and Sealand in 1965 (as L8) but only five minutes were saved and it reverted to its former status on 23rd March 1969 on which date a Saturday limited stop service from Woodside to Chester (L5) commenced at the expense of one journey per hour on the direct service C1. A weekday version deviating via Chester Zoo (L6) started three months later but it was liable to suspension if there was no demand. These journeys saved 10 minutes and attracted sufficient traffic to continue in operation for many years. A Heswall-Woodside limited stop peak hour service (L9) was started in January 1971

Rail Replacement Proposals

In 1966 British Railways proposed to withdraw the New Brighton-Wrexham train service and also to curtail the Hooton-Helsby service at Stanlow & Thornton. Crosville drew up a plan for a new service (F97) between Birkenhead and Wrexham via Heswall and Queensferry with one return journey running direct between Woodside and Queensferry (F98). For the Helsby closure they proposed to extend two-hourly trips on H24 Liverpool-Runcorn-Frodsham or Helsby to Woodside via Ellesmere Port thus creating a route with a journey time of 2½hours, the termini of which would be ¾mile apart and within sight of each other across the river. Neither of these closures was approved so these interesting schemes were scrapped.

Fares

By 1951, a fare increase, the first for over 20 years, could no longer be avoided and, in fact, fares rose twice in that year; the trend continued throughout that decade during which there were several increases in fuel tax. Workmen's day return tickets at single fare were replaced by work singles in the morning only and Crosville, like many other bus companies, changed over to the 5- or 6-day weekly ticket thus improving cash flow and weeding out the casual early travellers.

Because of different operating conditions and lower passenger density, company fares had always tended to be higher than municipal fares and, with successive increases, the gap widened. The municipalities adopted social policies with lower rates per mile for the longer distance passengers. Within their areas, Crosville had to match them but this created serious anomalies just beyond the points where municipal influence ended. Thus in 1966 it cost 11d to ride from Woodside to Eastham but 2/- (more than double) to Hooton Cross Roads, one mile beyond. The journey from Park Station to Frankby Green cost 9d but the charge to the next stage at Park Road, Newton was 1/8d, again more than double. Not unnaturally, the company's image suffered severely with the ordinary passenger, who did not understand the reasons for these apparent inequities. The coming of the PTE and the easing of the taper alleviated but failed to solve the problem entirely. Districts on the boundary of the PT Area such as Huyton and Rainhill enjoyed some concessions and even a few reductions for a time but the steep jump was merely moved further out from the city. The inflationary conditions of the seventies triggered fare increases which accelerated the decline of bus services. What was really happening was that bus fares were catching up on the increases which should have been made in the wartime and post-war period.

New in May 1951 as KG198, this shows the final form of the post-war half-cab Eastern Coach Works 39-seat rear-entrance bus body, being to the new 8ft width. Following the route renumbering of 1959, the original two-piece front destination indicators have been panelled over so that the top (destination) roll now carries route numbers and the lower aperture shows the destination. DLG198, which was caught by the camera in Banks Road, West Kirby, was withdrawn in 1967 and then served as a site office for a Warrington contractor.

Crosville hired ten of these Bristol MW6Gs from Red and White Services Ltd. of Chepstow in 1967-68. Dating from 1958-59, they were repainted in Crosville green for the duration of the hire but not given Crosville fleet numbers. U2359 (the 23rd underfloor-engined bus of 1959 in the Red and White system) is ready to leave West Kirby on a Capenhurst works service in December 1967.

This Bristol K6A with standard post-war Eastern Coach Works lowbridge body had a varied career having been one diverted to London Transport when new in 1949 until April 1950. When pictured in West Kirby in March 1961 it had had modified indicators fitted also standee windows which were not a normal feature. It was withdrawn in 1966 and scrapped.

Parkgate Esplanade has changed little over the years and this view of Lodekka DFB96 working a journey from West Kirby to Chester in February 1989 is taken from the opposite direction than that of M6 on page 33.

SRG62 was one of several dual-entrance Bristol RELL6Gs, seating 48 passengers which replaced double-deck buses on the West Kirby-Birkenhead and Wallasey services in 1968. They were among the last buses to have the route number indicator on the nearside. The small upper-case fleet name, used for a time in the late 'sixties, can just be discerned. This vehicle was withdrawn in 1981.

It was rare to see a Crosville bus displaying 'Hoylake' as a destination as the main terminals in the town were at Meols and West Kirby. Bristol L6B KW114 was diverted from the Caledonian Omnibus Co. in 1950 and is seen in Greasby on the short-lived service thence to Hoylake (King's Gap) via Pump Lane and Heron Road.

Vehicle exchanges for experimental purposes were not uncommon within the Tilling Group. United Automobile Services' BL45, a 1959 Lodekka LD6B with rear platform door, in Tilling red livery, stands at Woodside on a Chester via Ellesmere Port service in 1960. It was exchanged with DLB978, a similar Gardner-engined vehicle. The purpose of the exchange is unknown.

CHAPTER 7
POST-WAR LIVERPOOL

The company's first task in post-war Liverpool was to increase frequencies and restore late evening and Sunday services. From May 1946, the new Bristol K6A buses started appearing in substantial numbers, at first with gaping, empty destination boxes but gradually blinds were fitted, carrying a new set of route numbers for the public to memorise. For some time, both on the buses and in timetables, there was a strange mixture of old and new with new buses displaying route letters on Widd plates and numbers on their blinds. Timetables had such headings as 'Service A No.120'. Liverpool Corporation obligingly displayed the new route numbers on the stop signs in the city centre for which they had always borne responsibility. The new numbers, with the old letters in parenthesis, and the basic frequencies in the summer of 1947, were as below but the letters were still used internally and by the staff for more than 20 years.

116	Pier Head-Prescot via Roby & Huyton Quarry (F) 20 mins.
116A	Pier Head-Prescot via Roby & Windy Arbour Road (Cronton Avenue) (F) 2-hourly.
116B	Pier Head-Prescot via Huyton Village & Huyton Lane (F1) hourly
117	Pier Head-Gateacre-Tarbock-Widnes (E) 2-hourly
118	Pier Head-Gateacre-Halewood-Widnes (D) 2 - hourly
119	Pier Head-Prescot-Rainhill-Warrington (G & H) 20 mins. Rainhill Stoops, hourly Warrington
120	Pier Head-Speke-Widnes-Warrington (A) 20 mins.
121	Pier Head-Woolton-Hunts Cross-Halebank (C) 30 mins.
123	Pier Head-Cronton Colliery.

Both 116 and 120 had quarter-hourly services on Saturday afternoons and there was peak hour augmentation on most routes, including a local service between Pier Head and Gateacre for which Corporation buses were sometimes hired.

Joint Services

Crosville had always fought shy of involvement in joint services with other operators but events in 1947 forced the company into two alliances with St. Helens Corporation. In the previous year, the latter had started services between St. Helens and Speke (89) or Garston (90) which had been intended to be joint with Liverpool Corporation. However, the companies proved that the 1931 and 1938 Agreements had established their right to run services between St. Helens and anywhere in the city of Liverpool, not just the city centre, so Liverpool was debarred from participating. St. Helens ran the services alone with protection for Crosville route 116B between Prescot and Huyton until 2nd February 1947 when the Garston service was abandoned and a half-hourly joint service commenced between St. Helens and Speke, worked by Crosville and St. Helens buses with an 8% dormant Ribble share. The route number 89 had been chosen to fit in with Liverpool's series but Crosville perversely numbered it 137. It was some years before the necessary legend was put on the blinds and 89 was then displayed though 137 still appeared in the timetables.

Meanwhile, St. Helens and Warrington Corporations desired to run a direct all day service between the two towns via Bold Heath and Great Sankey, the then-existing service being the Ribble-St. Helens Corporation-Lancashire United joint Warrington-Southport route which then ran via Burtonwood and Cow Lane, Sankey. St. Helens already held a licence for a workmen's service over the Bold Heath route which had been introduced on 19th March 1944 with a nominal Lancashire United interest. To protect its interests, which dated back to 1921, Crosville demanded a share and a tripartite joint service (140) started on 31st August 1947. The service was somewhat irregular in frequency but eventually became every 90 minutes, hourly on Saturdays. The 90-minute service needed only one bus but all three operators participated at various times. Problems arose in March 1953 when Cow Lane was closed to permit extensions at Burtonwood US Air Base and the Warrington-Southport service, in which Crosville had no interest, was diverted over the 140 route, the latter being reduced more or less to a peak hour service. Matters were resolved in June 1955 when, following road improvements, the Southport service was rerouted via Winwick. In 1954 Crosville was asked to run workers' buses to Burtonwood and services 156 from Liverpool via Prescot and 157 from Garston via Widnes were put on. The latter was curtailed at Widnes by 1959 and both were withdrawn on 27th November 1959.

After pressure from the local authorities, the Liverpool-Warrington via Cronton and Farnworth service was restored after its wartime suspension on 11th December 1949. It now ran through to the Pier Head as service No. 143 instead of terminating at Wavertree and had a journey time of 69 minutes necessitating a frequency of 75 minutes, making it difficult for the public to memorise bus times. This state of affairs continued until 1958 when it was rerouted direct via Edge Lane with limited stops instead of the traditional Crosville route via Wavertree and Chatham Place. The journey time was reduced to 59 minutes and an hourly service was provided with crew changes on each trip. This was now the fastest bus service between Liverpool and Warrington.

Huyton, Whiston and Prescot

During the fifties many new housing estates were built in Huyton-with-Roby, Prescot and Whiston. The first two Urban

Bristol K6A MB254 was numerically the fourth new post-war Crosville double-deck bus with standard Tilling-group Eastern Coach Works lowbridge body seating 27/28. It is shown in original livery with cream upper-deck window surrounds, a feature which soon disappeared, and a full set of destination and route blinds for Liverpool-Prescot service 116. The bodies were built from unseasoned wood and MB254 was given a similar 1949 body taken from a 1932 Leyland TD2 M30 when the latter was withdrawn in February 1956.

An unusual view of a Liverpool Corporation AEC Regent II (A357) duplicating a Crosville bus on service 117. The Corporation had taken delivery of buses for tramway conversions and was able to help the company at a time of a serious double-deck bus shortage in 1949. The 'on hire' label can just be discerned in the bulkhead window. The Crosville bus is one of the first post-war Bristol K6As with 55-seat Eastern Coach Works bodies placed in service in May 1946 (MB259). It has already lost the original cream upper deck window surrounds.

The last 12 of the pre-war order for Leyland TD5 lowbridge double-deckers with Eastern Coach Works 52-seat bodies were not delivered until 1940 and M94 was ten years old when caught by the camera at the Pier Head after it had been equipped with standard Tilling two-part destination equipment at the front. It still sports the three cream bands of pre-war days. Note the rather basic wartime tubular steel passenger shelter, guaranteed to give protection only from vertical rain!

The earlier Bristol Lodekka LD6B buses had a very deep radiator grille as demonstrated by No. ML768 (later DLB768) seen taking layover at Bridge Foot, Warrington in March 1956 while working service 120 from Liverpool via Speke and Widnes. It was new in 1955, being one of the last to have the full length (49in) upper destination indicator. However the role of the blinds has been reversed, the upper aperture displaying an intermediate point and the lower one showing the ultimate destination. The bus still has the upper cream band which was shortly to disappear.

District Councils adopted a joint policy, mainly directed at what they considered to be Crosville's inadequate services. In Huyton there were problems because the operating boundary between the company and Liverpool Corporation ran almost through the town centre, preventing the logical extension of services. The Council wanted an internal circular service which would enable people to get to the Town Hall and shop in Huyton village and eventually Liverpool Corporation and Crosville, after resisting for some time, agreed to run it for an experimental period of one year. It started on 16th March 1953 as service 70, linking Page Moss, Woolfall Heath and Long View with Huyton centre. It needed one bus which ran hourly in each direction; Crosville seems to have run it on Saturdays only. As expected, the service failed to cover its costs and was withdrawn on 15th May 1954. So ended the only joint service between Liverpool Corporation and Crosville.

An industrial estate was being built at Wilson Road (Harold Wilson was Huyton's MP), just off Crosville's Huyton Quarry route, and special workers' journeys started on 5th July 1953 on which date service 116 was diverted through Manor Farm estate instead of St. John's Road. A further service into this district between the Pier Head and Elizabeth Road (168) commenced in 1955. The Council, with some justification, thought it unreasonable that workers needed to change buses at Archway Road en route from the housing estates along Liverpool Road which were less than two miles from the industrial area as the crow flies. Crosville refused to provide a service whereupon Liverpool agreed to run it from November 1954, with protection to the company between Archway Road and the industrial estate.

There was both residential and industrial development in Prescot and St. Helens Corporation had staked a claim in the Cross Lane Estate in 1949. In 1955, hourly journeys between Liverpool and Rainhill on 119 were diverted via Manchester Road and Bridge Road, avoiding Prescot centre, and an increasing number of journeys on 116 were diverted via Cross Lane, not only to serve the Cable Works, but to link new housing with both Prescot and Liverpool. The diverted 119 trips were renumbered 169 in December 1955. New housing in the area as a whole necessitated increased services on all the routes. By 1959, the Huyton Quarry service was running every 15-20 minutes, Windy Arbour Road every hour (half-hourly on Saturdays) and the Huyton Lane service had additional hourly trips to Whiston Lane which eventually were run through to Prescot, all buses being diverted through the Mosscroft Farm Estate from April 1961. Buses to Rainhill ran every 15 minutes with a once hourly trip via Manchester Road; on Saturdays there were two such trips on an irregular five-trips-an-hour service. Rainhill Stoops was also linked with St. Helens by a joint service (79) which commenced in April 1965.

When all Crosville routes were renumbered from 5th July 1959, Liverpool and Warrington depot routes were numbered in the 'H' series, virtually every variation being given a separate number and ending the confusion caused by so many different 116 services in Huyton.

Runcorn Bridge

The population in the once-rural districts between south

A contrast in Bristol Lodekka styling is demonstrated by No. DFG26, a 1960 FS6G with Cave-Brown-Cave heating and ventilation system and no radiator grille, which has had its destination equipment simplified, and 1956 LD6G No. DLG799 with a normal radiator grille and full destination layout though the upper aperture has been reduced to 41in. The scene is Liverpool Pier Head on 4th August 1962.

Liverpool and Widnes was also expanding, particularly in Hunts Cross, Halewood and Hough Green and, by 1959, the Hunts Cross service had an hourly extension to Halewood and both Widnes routes had hourly services, the Tarbock Green route being doubled on Saturdays. As the Halewood housing estates developed, Liverpool Corporation was authorised to run a competing service despite Crosville objections and, for a time, the district was overserved. Crosville buses were diverted on to Leathers Lane instead of Baileys Lane from September 1965.

The new road bridge between Widnes and Runcorn, replacing the old-fashioned Transporter Bridge, was opened on 21st July 1961, enabling Crosville to link up two separated parts of its network. The relocation of Liverpool overspill in Runcorn New Town generated a demand for through facilities and the company devised a complex system of through routes between Liverpool and Chester by extending the Halewood and Widnes services across the new bridge. This brought one Chester depot bus and six from Runcorn depot on to the Liverpool services for the first time. The new services started about 5.30pm on the opening day and were based on a 12-hour operating cycle within which each bus ran two return trips from Liverpool to Chester (H20 and H23) and one to Frodsham (H24). Services were reduced in the evenings. An industrial service (H25) between Liverpool and Runcorn via Speke replaced and extended some short journeys on the Warrington service (H1) and in October 1962, a further works service (H6) was inaugurated between Liverpool and Runcorn ICI offices via Huyton, Farnworth and Widnes.

From 1st November 1971 Widnes Corporation services from Whiston, Rainhill, Farnworth and Bold Heath ran through to Shopping City and became joint with Crosville as services J61-3. The J61 is the ancestor of Halton Transport service 61 between Murdishaw and Liverpool. The new Ford Factory at Speke and the old-established Dunlop factory provided some works traffic from Widnes and Runcorn. A service from Runcorn to the Ford works (H30) started on an 8-week unforeseen service licence on 8th April 1963 and lasted some time until the inevitable increase in lift-clubs killed the demand. The service number H29 was allocated to a service from Warrington to the Ford Works but it is not certain that it actually started. A few H1 and H25 through trips would deviate via the Dunlop factory to pick up small numbers of workers.

Traffic Congestion

As car ownership increased, congestion in Liverpool city centre at peak periods caused serious delay to bus services. Much of the problem was caused by vehicles queuing to enter the Tunnel and various traffic management schemes were devised during the sixties to alleviate the difficulties. In August 1965, London Road and Islington became one-way streets, taking the Prescot Road buses away from the London Road shopping area which gradually died. In May 1966 Dale Street became one way inward and the Corporation services affected switched to Chapel Street and Tithebarn Street outward. Crosville did not favour this route which served only the commercial district and rerouted the Prescot Road services H2, 3 and 4 via Church Street and Lime Street on the outward journey while retaining the Dale Street route inward. Flyovers, brought into use in 1969-70

Bristol VR DVG274, new in 1975, climbs Lord Street, Liverpool en route from Prescot to the Pier Head, with St. John's Beacon in the background. It has the curved windscreen fitted to the later VRs but lacks the PTE logo borne by most of its kind in the city.

The only low bridge in the Liverpool area which was seriously obstructive to buses was at Halebank station, closed in 1958. The close interworking of the Liverpool-Runcorn-Chester services H21-24 precluded the use of Bristol VRs on any of them though only H21 passed under the bridge and single-deck buses had to be used when OMO came along. The bridge decapitated several buses (none of them Crosvilles) including Liverpool Atlantean L677 which subsequently became an open top bus at Southport.

Bristol MW6G EMG435 was new in 1962, one of 10 coaches with the later style of ECW body with stepped waistrail, fluorescent lighting, curved roof lights, wrap-round corner windows and a Cave-Brown-Cave heating system. Their roof lights were replaced by fibreglass panels in the mid-sixties and they were cascaded to dual-purpose status and reclassified from CMG to EMG. The locale of the photograph is Barrow Street, St. Helens, on the joint service to Warrington shared with Warrington and St.Helens Corporations though the latter had been absorbed by Merseyside PTE a few days before this picture was taken in April 1974.

At one time only the oldest buses were allocated to colliery services but all that had changed by April 1978 when 10-year old Bristol RE CRG38 was caught in Huyton, in white National livery, working the Cronton Colliery-Mann Island service. The following year this 47-seat vehicle was equipped for one-man operation, repainted green and cream and downgraded to dual-purpose status; it was withdrawn in 1981.

The 8ft wide Eastern Coach Works lowbridge bodies on the 1952-53 Bristol KSW6B buses gave them a rather squat appearance. This was the last class to have the unpopular bench seats on the upper deck. MW491 (later DKB491) takes layover at Liverpool Pier Head between trips on the Huyton (Elizabeth Road) service.

solved most of the traffic congestion and the reduction of city centre jobs during the seventies did the rest.

There was a chronic staff shortage in the sixties and services, particularly on summer Saturdays, were unreliable, priority being given to covering the Warrington and Chester routes. Gaps of 90 minutes were not unknown on the Huyton and Halewood services. Car ownership in Liverpool and Huyton was lower than in Wirral, and there was so much new development in Crosville's operating area, the decline in traffic was slower than on the Cheshire side of the river. Although the company's traffic in the calendar year 1969 had fallen to 107.4 million passengers from a peak of 193.4 million in 1950 (55.5%) it must be remembered that whole areas in North and Central Wales had been virtually abandoned. The 67 vehicles based at Liverpool depot in 1947 had increased to about 100, including coaches. The revenue from the Liverpool services had always been essential to enable others in the rural areas to continue, but the point had now been reached when there were insufficient margins to continue cross-subsidisation.

CHAPTER 8

THE PTE YEARS 1969-86

In 1964, 13 years of Conservative rule came to an end and the incoming Labour government began applying new transport policies with a distinct socialist flavour. By this time, the bus industry was in a parlous state, beset by declining patronage, traffic congestion and serious labour shortages. Some municipal and county treasuries were already supporting many operators to avoid the total withdrawal of services.

By 1967 the formation of Conurbation Transport Authorities was being discussed as was the sale of the BET bus interests to the government who already held substantial shareholdings in many companies, inherited from the railway companies in 1947. The outcome was the passing of the Transport Act 1968, the formation of the National Bus Company (which commenced work on 1st January 1969, taking both Crosville and Ribble under its wing) and the creation of the first four Passenger Transport Authorities, of which Merseyside was one. The Liverpool, Birkenhead and Wallasey undertakings were taken over on 1st December 1969.

The Act laid down a new structure of grants to support both bus and rail services; on Merseyside these were administered by the Passenger Transport Authority (PTA) which comprised representatives of the 18 local authorities in the region and of the central government. Management was performed by the Passenger Transport Executive (PTE), a statutory body with powers of its own. Powers in the Act enabling the PTEs to become licensing authorities were not activated and it remained for each PTE to come to terms with the company operators in its area. In Manchester and Birmingham they were bought out while on Tyneside and Merseyside, agency agreements were negotiated.

In the meantime, Crosville continued to operate very much as before. It has been suggested that the companies dragged their feet in reducing services during the negotiation period in order to qualify for a greater share of the mileage but, in fact, there were a number of changes during this period, particularly on the Liverpool side of the river. A new Agreement was implemented on 30th January 1972 under the provisions of which Crosville would operate within the Passenger Transport Area as an agent for the PTE, all revenue being held in trust for the PTE which would meet the operating costs. These and formulae for dealing with cross-boundary traffic were set out in complex appendices to the Agreement. Crosville's share was 13.402% of the total mileage in the area.

In theory, this mileage could be worked on any service but, in practice, worker objections tended to keep Crosville buses on traditional routes in Liverpool though in Wirral, after very lengthy talks, greater flexibility was achieved.

Liverpool

From 30th January 1972 Crosville buses were able to carry local traffic within the city of Liverpool at the same fares as the PTE buses but, to avoid the need to allow extra running time, Crosville buses observed limited stops between the Pier Head and the outskirts. Stops used by Crosville buses were specially marked and the brand name *Merseyfare* was used to market the facility. The ultimate objective was to abolish the limited stops as services were altered and needed to be rescheduled anyway and this was eventually done. Buses on routes H1 and H25 used the PTE route via Leece Street and Catharine Street instead of Upper Duke Street and Canning Street and, whilst this was a minor change, it marked the final demise of the back street route policy which the Corporation had imposed in the twenties.

The PTE's policy was to make maximum use of the railways and achieve 100% one-man operation on the buses as soon as possible. The company was not much affected by the former though a special peak hour feeder service, (H99) between Mosscroft Farm Estate and Huyton Station commenced on 18th September 1972 as part of the PTE's demonstration programme. The experiment was deemed to be a success and the service continued to operate until June 1986.

As far as one-man operation was concerned, Crosville had already made some progress though the widespread use of Bristol Lodekkas in Liverpool, many of which had plenty of life left in them, inhibited rapid progress. Crosville's duties on route 79 and some on 140 had been converted in 1969 and one-man dual purpose Seddons had taken over H12/13 (Liverpool-Prescot via Windy Arbour Road) on 20th June 1971. Johnson Fare Boxes were used with no tickets but the PTE eventually demanded that they be removed as revenue control was poor. The opening of Runcorn Shopping City resulted in a revision of the Runcorn bridge services from 31st October 1971 with one-man single-deckers taking over many duties.

Huyton Rationalisation

There had been some discussion between Liverpool Corporation, Crosville and Huyton-with-Roby UDC in 1968 to seek a solution to the district's transport problems and, at the same time, to reduce the unprofitable services of both concerns. No agreement was reached and, in view of the impending formation of the PTE, the matter was placed in abeyance. Huyton was selected as the first district for a rationalisation scheme and, with the PTE making precepts on the rates, the Council now had to face up to the realities of transport costs. From 22nd October 1973, Crosville services H14 (Prescot via Huyton Lane) and H16 (Huyton, Elizabeth Road) were withdrawn, the former being replaced by the extension to Prescot of PTE service 76 which was transferred to Crosville and the latter by extending PTE service 40. Service H11 was renumbered H7 to avoid confusion with PTE service 11 which also ran into Huyton. These events were co-ordinated with the provision of services to the new Lickers Lane Estate, Whiston. H12 was at first diverted through the estate but was quickly restored to its original route as pensioners complained they could no longer reach the post office. There was also an hourly single-deck one-man service H18 between Prescot and Huyton Station via Lickers Lane during the daytime on weekdays only and a few peak hour trips to Liverpool (H15) which took the direct route via Edge Lane. These services were not entirely satisfactory and, from March 1974, one journey per hour on H8 was also rerouted via Lickers Lane.

The provision of a service between Prescot and Huyton only continued a trend which had originated with the inception of the Elizabeth Road service in 1955 when one bus had provided a shuttle service in Huyton on Saturday afternoons; H8 and H13 got a Saturday shuttle in 1969 and as the PTE pursued its pro-rail policy, the process was to gain momentum. In 1978 the arrangements were changed so that all Lickers Lane journeys ran through to Pier Head as H6 and a daytime local ran between Prescot and Huyton via Whiston Hospital and Huyton Quarry as H9. The Huyton Industrial Estate had expanded considerably, its location close to the M57 and M62 junction contributing to its growth. The special industrial journeys formerly numbered H9-10 were now renumbered H7X and H8X. H7-7X were diverted via Huyton Hey Road, and Huyton town centre in 1980. When a link road was built between the estate and the motorway roundabout, buses on the Windy Arbour Road service H13 did a double-run between Cronton Road and Huntley and Palmer's at factory times.

Double-deck one-man operation had been adopted on the Liverpool-Rainhill/Cronton-Warrington services H2-3/5 in December 1976. Later when a weight restriction was placed on the railway bridge in Bridge Road, Prescot, the Manchester Road journeys H4 were abandoned except for one works trip. Buses on H7/7X ran non-stop along Manchester Road to the bus station until rescheduled four years later. The similar conversion of the Liverpool-Huyton-Prescot services H6-9 was planned for 17th June 1979 but delayed for four days by a strike. H12-13 were now interworked and converted from single-deck to double-deck operation. Crosville workings on 89, St. Helens-Speke were also converted on the same day, the PTE St. Helens depot workings having been changed over in January. As an extra PTE bus was needed to maintain the same time-

A notable landmark and traffic centre on both the Huyton and Widnes groups of services was Wavertree Clock Tower (or the Picton Clock after its 1884 donor). Bristol VRT DVG282 passes by en route from Pier Head to Prescot via Huyton Quarry.

table, the economies were minimal. A year later, alternate journeys on this route were diverted to Halewood instead of Speke as 89A.

Halewood and Runcorn

As mentioned earlier, Liverpool Corporation had superimposed their own service (78) on Crosville's local service between Liverpool and Halewood in 1965. Simultaneously with the 1973 Huyton changes, Crosville service H19 between Pier Head, Hunts Cross and Halewood (which was almost identical to the 78) was withdrawn and an hourly H20 journey to Runcorn followed the route through Gateacre and Halewood. The H21 continued to go to Chester via Hunts Cross. There were other minor changes to the Runcorn services which were now fully one-man operated. In the course of a further timetable revision in June 1979, limited stop working along Wavertree Road ceased on services H20-24.

Frequencies on these services were reduced in October 1980, H24 being withdrawn in the evenings and on Sundays and mostly curtailed to run between Liverpool and Widnes. H22, Liverpool-Frodsham was abandoned and replaced by some extra trips on H20. The Liverpool-Runcorn via Speke peak hour service H25 was given a regular daytime service at the expense of trips on H1 to Warrington, the frequency of which was reduced from 20 minutes to hourly. The H1 and 76 were now the only two services worked by Lodekkas with conductors and they were finally converted to one-man operation with VRs on 29th March 1981.

On 1st December 1985, a Town Lynx limited stop service between Murdishaw, Runcorn Shopping City, Widnes and Liverpool (X5) was started providing a fast through service using the Duple Laser bodied Tiger coaches displaced from the Ellesmere Port-Liverpool service X7 (see below). This successfully reversed the decline in traffic and, by penetrating the residential areas, gained traffic from rail.

Special Services

Crosville's Liverpool depot suffered considerably from labour troubles during this period and in several years the PTA/PTE Annual Reports referred to excessive mileage lost by Crosville due to industrial action. The slightest incident was met by a work stoppage and the inflexibility of the staff made it difficult to allocate the correct proportion of mileage to the company. When the International Garden Festival was held on reclaimed land between Dingle and Aigburth in 1984, the PTE allocated two Crosville and two Ribble buses to the special service 401 between Pier Head and the Festival Grounds. Two 1970 Daimler Fleetlines with 71-seat Northern Counties bodies (HDG910/4), purchased from Southdown, were finished in the special Festival livery, the stand-by being another second-hand vehicle, ex-South Yorkshire PTE Bristol VR HVG933.

The same type of vehicle was also used on a contract service allocated to Crosville by the PTE between Lime Street Station and Brocklebank Dock in connection with the Dublin steamers.

A New Depot

Despite sundry improvements in the sixties and seventies, Crosville's Edge Lane depot was in great need of modernisation. Its situation over three miles from the city terminus was far from ideal and for some years the company had leased premises, at first in Wapping and later in Maddrell Street, off Gt.Howard Street, for carrying out minor mechanical adjustments during the day. As the Edge Lane premises were hemmed in, it was decided to seek premises nearer the city centre and on 3rd August 1985 Edge Lane depot was closed and the company moved to premises in Love Lane on the north side of the city centre. The depot was rented from the Merseyside Development Corporation, having originally been Tate and Lyle's transport depot. The Edge Lane premises were sold and demolished, a DIY supermarket being built on the site. Being much closer to the Pier Head terminus at Mann Island, the new site was much more economical for driver changeovers, staff usually being conveyed to and from the depot in one of the second-hand double-deckers. However, it was far from convenient for changeovers on service 89 which were done at Archway Road, Huyton. The PTE was not prepared to pay for the excessive dead mileage involved and consequently before Edge Lane depot closed, the Crosville share of 89/89A was transferred to Ribble who,

Following the success of Merseyside PTE's New Brighton-Liverpool service through the second Mersey road tunnel, a second cross-river service between Heswall and Liverpool city centre, using part of the M53 motorway, was allocated to Crosville Heswall depot. Bristol RELL6G ERG288 with 50-seat dual-purpose ECW body is seen in Tithebarn Street. The popularity of the service soon justified the substitution of double-deck buses of which Bristol VR DVG265, displaying a PTE 'Rapidride' board, was typical.

Merseyside PTE's road-rail integration plans included a peak hour feeder between Mosscroft Farm and Huyton Station (H99) on which 11.3m Leyland National ENL849 is seen promoting the humble potato.

Six Bristol VRs with East Lancs. bodies were bought from South Yorkshire PTE in 1980; they were third hand having originated with Sheffield Transport Dept. in 1972. HVG933 is working as a relief bus on the special service to the International Garden Festival in 1984. Its normal duties included the Lime Street Station - Brocklebank Dock contract for the Dublin vessels (for which additional luggage accommodation was provided) and ferrying drivers between Love Lane depot and Mann Island.

Huyton Industrial Estate brought extra traffic and some problems in the sixties and seventies. The suffix letter X was allocated in 1978 for trips on services H7 and H8 to, from or via Wilson Road. DFG64 was a 1961 Bristol FSF6G with 70-seat ECW body, sold early in 1979.

Ribble 1975 Leyland Atlanteans 1301 and 1369 were hired for a time and the latter, temporarily numbered DAL769, is seen in Whitechapel on the Warrington via Cronton service, followed by a Bristol Lodekka. This street is now pedestrianised.

Bridge Foot, Warrington was the eastern extent of Crosville's Merseyside operations. Originally buses stood on the east side of the bridge in Mersey Street together with North Western and Lancashire United buses and their joint operators but moved to the west side late in the 1939-45 War. It was not until 1956 that the move to Arpley Station was made. Bristol VR DVL386, seen on the Liverpool via Farnworth and Cronton service on 1st April 1979 is probably from Warrington depot as it does not bear the Merseyside PTE logo.

Certain of the eleven Dennis Loline III buses with Alexander 71-seat bodies, taken over with the mid-Cheshire services of the original North Western Road Car Co., were occasionally seen in Liverpool on workings from Warrington depot. DEG402 was originally placed in service in December 1961 as North Western 897 and was sold to a dealer in 1978. The Loline was really a Bristol Lodekka built by Dennis under licence as the state-owned Bristol works could not sell its products outside the Tilling group.

The purchase of Seddons by Crosville in 1971-72 caused quite a stir. Half the order for 100 vehicles, all with Seddon bodywork, were dual-door 45-seat buses like SPG779 seen on the Park Station-Greasby-West Kirby service in the Spring of 1978. The Seddons apparently did not stand up to Crosville conditions too well and SPG779 was one of 17 withdrawn in 1980.

it will be recalled, had an 8% share in the service but had never operated. The most economical way to work it was from Wigan depot as buses could work on service between Wigan and St. Helens, the only dead mileage being on the last trip at night which finished at Halewood and the bus then had to run empty to Wigan. Ribble used Leyland Nationals on this service.

Wirral Services

Wirral's transport problems were different from those of Liverpool where company buses traversed well-defined corridors. In Wirral Crosville was more or less everywhere and lightly-loaded, heavily restricted buses were duplicating local buses, creating a very wasteful situation. There was not only a need to integrate the Crosville services with the former municipal routes but also to break down the barriers between the two ex-Corporation systems. Furthermore, the network as a whole, being ferry-oriented was out-of-date and needed thorough investigation to ascertain modern needs.

As in Liverpool, restrictions on the carriage of local traffic in Birkenhead and Wallasey were removed from 30th January 1972 and the Merseyfare limited stop principle was applied to the former restricted sections of route. This was accepted by men at West Kirby and Heswall depots but not at Rock Ferry where the road staff insisted on clinging to the old arrangements. Thus no local traffic was carried on New Chester Road nor on Borough Road as the Parkgate service was worked from Rock Ferry. The Heswall men supported the Rock Ferry men over common sections. It was not until 3rd September 1972 that the Agreement was fully implemented.

An immediate result of impending PTE financial support was the commencement of an off-peak weekday local service between Parkgate, Neston and Little Neston (F14-16) in November 1971. Otherwise there was no change to the network. The peak hour Heswall-Woodside limited stop service L9 was replaced by an all-day weekday service between Heswall and Liverpool from 10th December 1973. Numbered in the PTE's Rapidride series, 418-9, it ran via the M53 and Wallasey Tunnel and followed different routes through Liverpool City Centre at peak and off-peak times. With an hourly service all day stepped up to half-hourly at the peaks; this service, which was run by Crosville, was an immediate success and was later increased in frequency and converted to double-deck operation using hired PTE Daimler Fleetlines painted in Crosville livery.

The first relatively minor rationalisation moves took place in February 1974 when Crosville's F7 between Woodside and Mill Park was withdrawn in favour of a PTE peak hour Rapidride service 441 and the company took over operation of PTE service 44 between New Ferry and Eastham Ferry. The PTE had closed its New Ferry depot in 1973 and the 44 was expensive to operate from Laird Street. It was really a homecoming as the 44 had been one of the services transferred to Birkenhead Corporation in 1930. At the same time the F15 Woodside-Willaston-Burton service was diverted to call at Neston Station in furtherance of the PTE's pro-rail policy and the F17-18 Woodside-Parkgate service was diverted via Mount Road estate in lieu of Thornton Road, enabling PTE service 84 to be withdrawn. The Woodside-Irby Mill Hill-Caldy-Meols service (F27) was rerouted through Greasby and Mill Lane, leaving Arrowebrook Lane without a bus service and setting the scene for the later withdrawal of PTE route 78 (Woodside-Greasby). In 1977, F27 was rerouted direct from Greasby to Farmers Arms via Frankby instead of Irby Mill Hill.

The other major change was an hourly service on the C22-23 Chester-Meols service, every third trip being on the C23 route via Willaston. This was a substantial increase in frequency which was to some extent compensated by the curtailment of F40-41, New Ferry-West Kirby at Heswall where there were good connections with C22-23.

There had been some one-man operation in Wirral since the late fifties when some Bristol L half-cab single-deckers had been fitted with jack-knife doors and modified bulkheads. From 5th October 1969, the Woodside-Parkgate service and Ellesmere Port locals F64-66 had been converted and in 1971-72 some Heswall and West Kirby routes were changed over using Seddons. Now all remaining duties at Rock Ferry depot were converted except those on the Birkenhead-Chester services C1 and C3-4 and some school journeys. C1 became one-man on 1st August 1976, initially using six Bristol VR double-deck and two Leyland National single-deck buses, and C3-4 in April 1978.

Revised PTE and Company Boundaries

From 1st April 1974 the Merseyside County Council was formed and became the transport authority for the region. Neston, having been amalgamated with Ellesmere Port in a new Borough, was excised from the Passenger Transport Area and henceforth became the responsibility of Cheshire County Council. Coincidentally, a new bus station was opened in Wellington Road, Ellesmere Port in April 1974 and control of the sub-depot which had been established there two years earlier was transferred from Rock Ferry to Chester. This move was in readiness for a divisional reorganisation on 1st July 1974 when six administrative areas were replaced by four. The Merseyside division was renamed 'North' and took in Runcorn and Warrington depots.

Full Integration Achieved

After very long and difficult negotiations between the PTE and the unions, a scheme which fully integrated the Crosville services in Wirral with those of the PTE was put into effect on 1st April 1979, resulting in a saving of 25 buses. All Crosville services which were wholly or mainly in the PTE area were given route numbers in the PTE series between 72 and 89. Thus Heswall services F19-26, which were otherwise unchanged were numbered 72-79 in the same order. It was decided that with only one exception Crosville and PTE buses should not both run on the same routes and this caused the biggest changes which were on the West Kirby services. It was agreed that PTE buses would serve the route through Moreton while Crosville buses would exclusively operate the routes through Greasby and Frankby. The Liscard-West Kirby and Park Station-Moreton-West Kirby sections were served by PTE routes 7, 8 and 28 which had hitherto terminated in Moreton, giving through services from New Brighton and Bromborough.

All the Greasby/Frankby services ran from Woodside, 80-80A via Prenton Dell and Arrowe Park (absorbing PTE services 78, 80 and Crosville F27); 81 via Park Station (replacing Crosville services F32 and part of F34) and 82 via Claughton Road (replacing PTE service 96 and part Crosville F32/34). Between Frankby and West Kirby, three routes were served, via Caldy (80), via Newton and Column Road (80A, 82 and also 85 – see below) and via Greenbank Road (81). The exceptions to the exclusive rule were on route 80 where PTE buses (80B) ran short journeys to Prenton Dell and Arrowe Park at certain times and the West Kirby-Saughall Massie-Park Station service which was covered by extending the PTE Port Sunlight-Claughton Village service via Saughall Massie (51D) or via Pump Lane (51E), the last solitary journey bringing PTE buses briefly into Greasby.

The Chester-Meols service was cut short at West Kirby and reduced in frequency, the New Ferry-Heswall services F40-1 being replaced by a network of three services, 83 and 84 from New Ferry and 85 from Eastham Ferry to West Kirby. The 85 all but eclipsed the 44 which had only a few peak and depot journeys and the number was officially abandoned in 1983, depot journeys being designated 85C. These services were over-optimistically frequent and they underwent many changes. The New Ferry-West Kirby services (83-84) were withdrawn in December 1980 except for school and depot trips; some 85 journeys were rerouted through Raby as 85A to replace 84. An experiment to serve Brimstage village, which had had no bus service for some years, with these trips was carried out in 1982, with a double run along Brimstage Road but it was abandoned after less than two months because of reversing difficulties and lack of patronage. Hospital trips to Clatterbridge from Meols and New Ferry took the vacant numbers 86 and 86A respectively. In the same month the Chester-West Kirby services were re-extended to Meols.

Between Woodside and Rock Ferry, New Chester Road was served solely by Crosville buses on the Chester, Ellesmere Port and North Wales services, the latter (F9-11) being rerouted through Eastham Village to provide a token service. The F8 to Holywell had been abandoned in 1977 by which time the Loggerheads journeys had been diverted to Pantymwyn via Cadole. These services continued to decline being further reduced in 1983 and again in September 1984 when the Denbigh journeys ceased.

The F15 Woodside-Burton service was renumbered 89 and diverted via Old Chester Road, Lower Bebington, Spital and Mill Park; this indirect route made it very slow and unattractive; its remaining traffic was rapidly discouraged and it was totally abandoned on 7th December 1980. The Parkgate service F17-18 became 87-88 and was rerouted via Whetstone Lane and Church Road, Higher Tranmere instead of Borough Road.

Ellesmere Port and Neston

After 1974, Merseyside PTE and Cheshire County Council collaborated well in matters of revenue support and did not allow the artificial boundary between them to become a transport barrier. In December 1980, the Heswall-Lower Village-Gayton local circular (79) was joined with the Parkgate-Neston local services F14/16 to create two through services, F14 via Five Lane Ends and F16 via Parkgate and this was replaced in July 1982 by a through service from Woodside, calling at Arrowe Park Hospital, Pensby and Heswall (72C, 72D). Some off-peak journeys were extended to Ness (Denhall Lane) in June 1983 after the County Council had built a turning circle.

The new borough was itself rather artificial with two

This Bristol MW6G was new in June 1961, one of eight 39-seat coaches, painted in cream livery and fitted with Cave-Brown-Cave heating for which the inlets can be seen below the windscreen. In 1971, they were all fitted with 43 bus seats and adapted for one-man operation and reclassified from CMG to SMG. SMG411 is seen in West Kirby in May 1972 bound for Liscard, wearing the all green Tilling livery applied in 1971 with the lower-case fleet name style which immediately preceded the NBC corporate livery.

The Oldham registration number betrays this Seddon Pennine IV as a former demonstrator, new in 1974, purchased by Crosville the same year. Although allocated the vacant fleet number SPG699, ahead of the original Seddons, it had 49 superior seats and should, perhaps, have been an EPG. Note the cream relief on both the waist rail and the wheels despite an NBC ruling to paint vehicles all over green to save money. The bus has come from Chester and is about to descend the hill into West Kirby on 8th June 1975.

Bristol MW6G EMG433 was delivered in May 1962, one of a batch of 10 39-seat luxury coaches fitted with a new style of Eastern Coach Works body with wrap-round corner windows, fluorescent lighting, stepped waist-rail and Cave-Brown-Cave heating. They originally had curved glass roof lights but these were replaced by fibreglass panels between 1965 and 1967 and they were later downgraded to dual purpose vehicles. The scene is Caldy village in September 1972; note the Merseyfare board with the PTE emblem indicating that local passengers are now carried in Birkenhead.

towns with vastly differing characteristics, one on the Mersey and the other on the Dee, separated by a tract of countryside which was very much stockbroker belt. Ellesmere Port itself continued to expand in the seventies and eighties so that suburban sprawl engulfed the once separate villages of Whitby, Great Sutton and Little Sutton. The local bus network expanded and the Council supported a service (F59) between Ellesmere Port and Neston, connecting the two parts of the borough; this was extended to Ness at peak hours on 6th April 1980 when there was a thorough reorganisation of the Ellesmere Port services following a comprehensive survey. The new network was marketed under the local identity name TransPort which appeared on the locally based buses.

Despite its local status and one-man operation, the running time on the Birkenhead-Chester direct service was reduced from 62 to 53 minutes, two minutes less than its pre-war time and the services via Ellesmere Port (C3-4) were also accelerated, the former being diverted through the Hope Farm Estate at Whitby. There was a half-hourly service on C1 and a combined 15-minute service on C3-4, reduced to about half-hourly in the evenings and on Sundays. Many local services were revised and new residential areas served, particularly in Great Sutton.

Town Lynx

On 3rd December 1979 Crosville introduced the first of a network of limited stop services under the name *Town Lynx.* The original services ran from Runcorn Shopping City to Ellesmere Port and Queensferry and then either to Mold (X1) or Flint (X2) and are really no part of this story. They were worked by two Duple-bodied Leyland Leopard dual-purpose vehicles, ELL502 based at Runcorn depot and ELL503 based at Flint; they were finished in a two-tone green and white livery with a leaping Lynx motif, not dissimilar from the dual-purpose livery introduced in 1981. These services underwent several changes eventually becoming X1 Chester-Manchester.

A group of Bristol REs and Leyland Nationals in the overflow parking-ground in Greenbank Road, West Kirby in October 1980. Note the high proportion of dual-purpose vehicles, identifiable by their cream upper parts. The vehicle in the foreground, ERG56, was a 50-seater, new in June 1968.

From 4th April 1981, Crosville introduced a Town Lynx service (X5) on Saturdays from Caergwrle and Mold to Liverpool (Skelhorne Street bus station) via the M53 and from 13th June 1981, a further Saturday service (X7) was commenced between Ellesmere Port and Liverpool with three trips. On both services one afternoon trip was extended to Stanley Park for Liverpool or Everton football matches. The Caergwrle service was not a success being withdrawn on 26th September 1981 but the X7 continued. A Christmas shopping service was added on Tuesdays, Thursdays and Saturdays in December 1983 and, from June 1984, it was extended to the Garden Festival, but still running on Saturdays only.

An additional daily Chester-Liverpool X7 service running hourly on weekdays and 2-hourly on Sundays, via Ellesmere Port and M53 commenced on 9th November 1984, using new Leyland Tiger coaches with Duple Laser bodies, based at Chester and Ellesmere Port depots. The journey time of 53 minutes was the same as on the Chester direct service from Woodside and the new service provoked a one-day strike at Liverpool depot and considerable disruption at Rock Ferry, on the grounds of loss of work for the latter, though it had no effect on the Liverpool men. The daily service was successful and from 3rd November 1985 the Tigers were replaced by coach-seated Leyland Olympian double-deck vehicles (EOG 200-2).

The Revised Agreement

When the PTE's area had been enlarged in 1984, Crosville's mileage entitlement was reduced to 11.16%. The PTE was not happy about the Agreement as it believed that there was little or no incentive for the companies to make economies and that they gave Merseyside a low priority compared to other parts of their operating areas in such matters as one-man operation. The companies on their part deplored the PTE's 'one-man operation at any price' policy pointing out that assets could not be discarded without regard to the cost. The PTE gave one year's notice to end the Agreement in 1978 but there were several extensions of time whilst negotiations continued. A new Agreement was signed on 20th June 1984, back-dated to 17th May 1981.

Much greater control of company costs was given to the Executive and a Bus Council was formed with representatives of the PTE and the companies to review the county services three times per year. There was to be much tighter budgetary control. The schedules to this Agreement reveal that on the 1981 Commencement Date, Crosville was in debt to the National Bus Company to the extent of £4,605,800 and the PTE agreed to pay a proportion of the interest on this sum. It was a reflection of the changed fortunes of the company so many of whose services had been in sparsely populated parts of Wales, Cheshire and Shropshire. Meanwhile new legislation, aimed at abolition of the Merseyside County Council and privatisation of the bus industry gave rise to conditions of great uncertainty.

Patronage continued to decline, particularly in the evenings and on Sundays and there was a major reorganisation of the West Kirby services in December 1985 including the restoration of the circular service. New service numbers, 37, 38 and 39 were similar but not identical to the former Crosville numbers F37-9. Routes 37-37A ran between New Brighton and Woodside via West Kirby and Greasby whilst 38-39 were the circulars from Woodside back to Woodside. Crosville buses were back in Moreton and, in the evening they ran some trips to New Brighton, their first appearance there on service despite several attempts spanning 60 years. In June 1986 many services were cut down as a preparatory step towards the new era of deregulation, due to start on 26th October 1986. This resulted in the 38-39 circular being withdrawn in the evenings and on Sundays and the 80-80A Sunday frequency cut to 2-hourly.

In preparation for deregulation, the company abolished its divisional structure and replaced it with a number of Districts each of which had to stand or fall by its financial results. Liverpool and Wirral now became separate autonomous Districts.

Several Leyland Nationals were transferred to Crosville from the Northern General Transport Co. Ltd. of Gateshead during 1983-84. All but one were broken up for spares and the one which got away, SNG836, seen in Mold on the service from Birkenhead, is of special interest as it took over the fleet number of an earlier National ENL836 which was scrapped as a result of a serious accident. The broad cream band was a refreshing change from the all-over green livery which was the official NBC standard. The fleet number seems to have been unlucky as this bus caught fire on 6th November 1984 and was scrapped.

Leyland Olympian DOG110 was one of the first batch placed in service in late 1982. It has just climbed the hill from West Kirby *en route* for Heswall, Neston and Chester on 16th April 1983. Notice that it carries both the NBC and Merseyside PTE logos at either end of the fleet name.

Bristol RELL6G SRG185 was one of 20 dual-entrance 48-seat buses and is seen in Chester on the limited stop L5 from Woodside in July 1971. Note the curved windscreens and the fact that the route number has now been moved to the offside to facilitate control by the driver.

Leyland National ENL847, a 1973 48-seat dual-purpose vehicle, emerges from Arrowebrook Lane en route from West Kirby to Woodside on 24th February 1974, the last day before the F27 was diverted via Greasby village along the road to the right. On the left is the wooded splendour of Arrowe Park. The F27 was usually worked by dual-purpose vehicles, though they were likely to be replaced at weekends when demands on the express services were heavy.

Bristol VR DVL334 had apparently been the victim of a top deck arsonist when pictured in Greasby on 23rd July 1985. The photograph shows the neat, clean lines of the rear end of the Bristol VR compared to the rather fussy bustle styles of some other contemporary double-deck buses.

West Kirby Concourse on a clear winter's day in December 1982. Two Leyland Olympians and a National of Crosville and a Daimler Fleetline of Merseyside PTE stand, awaiting their respective departure times.

CHAPTER 9

THE LAST YEARS

The deregulation provisions of the Transport Act 1985 abolished virtually all controls on routes, timetables and fares; by giving six weeks' notice to the Traffic Commissioner anyone who could get an Operator's Licence could start a bus service to run at times and fares of his choice. The Transport Authority, i.e. the PTE or County Council, was debarred from subsidising any service if a competing service had been registered commercially or tenders had been considered. By the closing date for initial commercial registrations it was apparent that a few areas attracted no commercial services at all and large areas would be without commercial services early in the morning, in the evenings and on Sundays. These were the facilities which had to be put out to tender but first there was the difficult task of deciding what the reasonable needs of each route would be at these times.

The PTE then invited tenders for the provision of services considered necessary but, for practical reasons, often split these up into Early Morning, Late Evening and Sundays so that eventually two or three operators could work the same route at different times. The PTE made matters more complicated by retaining elements of its Cheap Fares Policy on tendered services so that there were two fare scales, one for commercial services and another for subsidised operations, the latter being identified by a Merseytravel board which it was obligatory for the operator to display. These subsidised services were distinguished by different route numbers usually, but not always, indicated by the normal service number plus 100.

Crosville tendered for a great number of these and was so successful on both sides of the river that there was some speculation that the bids had been set uneconomically low. In Liverpool, H1 (Warrington via Widnes), H2 (Warrington via Rainhill), H7-12 (Prescot via Windy Arbour Road) and 89 St.Helens-Speke were not registered, H1 being replaced by an increased service on H25 to Runcorn. The PTE and Cheshire County Council (Cheshirebus) thought that H2 was needed only between Prescot and Warrington and while Crosville got the contract for a 2-hourly service on Sundays (almost the same service as in 1921!), the weekday service went to Shearings. Few Liverpool services were registered commercially on Sundays, but Crosville won most of the tenders. The H-prefixed numbers did not readily adapt to the PTE's plus 100 scheme and whilst the tendered version of H6-8 became 106-8, H3 became 143.

Crosville won contracts for all-day services on some ex-Merseyside PTE services which Merseybus had not registered viz:

102 Norris Green-Walton-Croxteth Hall-Broad Green Hospital (½-hourly Daily)
111 Stockbridge Village-Alder Road-Green Lane-Pier Head (½-hourly Daily)
125 Walton-Everton-Grove Street-Princes Park-Garston (15-30 mins Daily)
130 Everton Valley-Netherfield Road-Pier Head (15-30 mins Daily)
135 Bootle (New Strand)-Gt.Howard St-Pier Head (Mann Island) (½-hourly off-peak)
173 Netherley-Belle Vale-Childwall-Ullet Road Pier Head (½-hourly Daily)
192 Halewood-Belle Vale-Huyton-Kirkby-Fazakerley-Walton (½-hourly Daily)

In addition, early or late and/or Sunday journeys were won on services between the city centre and Lyme Cross (129), Hall Road Station, Crosby (131), Knowsley Village (139), Litherland (Hatton Hill Road) (158), Hunts Cross (172) and Prescot (Thomas Drive) (197). A further success was the contract for transporting handicapped people in special vehicles owned by the PTE, which were adapted to carry wheelchairs.

Labour Problems

For many years, Crosville's Liverpool depot suffered from difficult labour relations, caused by domination of the union committee by a small group of militants who did not represent the views of the silent majority. Alarming tales are told of intimidation being used on staff who did not toe the line. Some men were permanently working to rule and, while management may not have been perfect, the company seems to have done its best in a difficult situation, sometimes with official union support. However, the hard-liners seemed to have a death-wish and, after deregulation, they could not, or would not, appreciate that the NBC financial rug had been pulled from beneath both the company and themselves. This was the background against which the events of late 1986 and early 1987 were played.

An example of the readiness of the drivers to strike was seen in May 1986, a few weeks after five new MCW Metroliner three-axle double-deck coaches had been allocated to Love Lane for use on National Express services to Manchester and Leeds via M62. In the course of these duties, Crosville drivers were required to drive similar vehicles belonging to East Yorkshire Motor Services Ltd. Liverpool depot staff had negotiated for a cab-door which was different even from those accepted for one-man operation by all other Crosville depots. Naturally, East

An impressive array of Leyland Olympians seen parked up at Heswall depot on Saturday, 23rd August 1986. A few years earlier every bus would have been on service on a Saturday afternoon.

Crosville and North Western joined forces in running a joint service between Banks, north-east of Southport and Chester via Liverpool and Crosville double-deck coach DOG202 turns out of Lime Street into Ranelagh Street to reach the St.John's Market loading point.

Two months after operations from Liverpool depot ceased, most of the local Crosville fleet was still in the yard at Love Lane. This picture, taken from a passing train on 16th March 1987 shows one of the ex-West Midlands vehicles which sparked the final work stoppage and at least one ex-PTE Fleetline among the Crosville VRs and Nationals.

Three liveries on display in a silent Love Lane depot yard on 22nd January 1987, a week after Crosville's Liverpool operations finally ceased. Left to right, Bristol VR DVG273 is in Brunswick green with orange roof. DVG275 is in National leaf green and cream while ex-West Midlands PTE VR HVG964 is still in that PTE's blue and cream. It was a dispute about driving the ex-West Midlands vehicles which led to closure of the depot. Note that the centre vehicle is displaying 'Everton Valley' on the blind, one of the destinations of service 130, gained under contract after deregulation.

Leyland Tiger CTL41 with 49-seat Duple Laser body, new in 1984, was one of several coaches finished in Town Lynx livery for use on the limited stop services between Runcorn and Liverpool

Leyland National SNL980, a 1977 model, had acquired North Western decals after the first stage of the break-up of Crosville in September 1989. It has just left Hood Street Gyratory on one of the limited stop services to Runcorn.

Yorkshire vehicles were not fitted with cab doors of this pattern and the union committee thought that, as a fair proportion of traffic was for cash, Liverpool-style doors should be fitted for security reasons. A strike was called whereupon the Metroliners were removed from Love Lane depot during the night and next day (5th June) they appeared on their normal duties, manned by Ribble drivers from Manchester depot. So much for solidarity! Crosville lost the work permanently and the only National Express mileage done was duplication, usually to Birmingham, using a Bristol RE, by that time a rare sight on such work.

Following the success of the company's tenders, many more men and vehicles were required at Liverpool depot and 100 additional drivers were recruited. Several Leyland Nationals were transferred from other depots and 36 Daimler Fleetlines were hired from Merseyside PTE. Some of these had been on loan to Crosville at Heswall in Crosville colours and had not long been returned to their owners, having been repainted in PTE livery by the company. Now they were back with Crosville, still in PTE colours with Crosville fleetnames and logos added. Unfortunately, they were past their best and there were continual mechanical troubles resulting in missed trips and many complaints from the PTE with fines being imposed. Some contracts were surrendered and in December 1986, 10 Bristol VRs ex-West Midlands PTE, were hired from dealers, Martins of Middlewich, and prepared for service at Rock Ferry. They retained their blue and cream livery with Crosville names and numbers added.

The union committee objected to there being no power-steering as there was a long-standing agreement that only volunteer drivers would be used on buses not so equipped but it was obviously not a proposition to pay £1,000 per bus to fit this refinement to buses on short-term hire. No one-man double-deckers without this feature had been operated in Liverpool previously and apparently management agreed to allocate them to part-day duties as far as practicable. There is no doubt that driving a one-man double-deck bus on city service with manual steering is quite hard work but these buses had been satisfactorily operated in the heavily-congested West Midlands since 1975. Furthermore, Merseyside PTE had run 60 Atlanteans without power steering since 1972. The union committee instructed members not to drive these buses and, on 5th January, when one of them was allocated to the first duty out in the morning, the driver refused to take it. He was suspended and the drivers struck. It was suggested by the union that the buses be distributed around all the depots and used only on part-day duties but this was turned down by the company. Work was resumed on 13th January on the understanding that negotiations would take place and the disputed vehicles would not be used. All the duties could not be covered on this basis and a compromise was reached that the buses would be used only on part-day duties. The union committee wanted to call a meeting to put this solution to the members but the company insisted on the agreement being implemented immediately and the strike was resumed on 15th. The company's view was that acquiescing to a scenario where drivers refused to take out roadworthy buses would lead to anarchy, possibly with serious repercussions at other depots. Furthermore, there was a well-established disputes procedure which had been completely ignored. The drivers were dismissed on 24th for engaging in illegal industrial action. There were short-lived strikes in support at other Crosville depots on 26th.

The strikers staged a sit-in at Love Lane for several days in late January but the company obtained a court order to evict them. Conciliation machinery was fully utilised and the affair was referred to NBC headquarters. There were rumours that Merseybus would take over the operations but these came to nothing though over half the dismissed drivers were eventually engaged by Merseybus.

Early in February, the Traffic Commissioner summoned Crosville to appear before him and the company, which had received fuel rebate for services which had not run for almost a month, was told that unless they resumed operations, their registrations would be cancelled. The Runcorn, Warrington and Chester Town Lynx services were restarted from those depots but an attempt to persuade the Rock Ferry men to operate H3, Liverpool-Rainhill Stoops, was unsuccessful.

Staff from other depots began removing buses from Love Lane, despite the presence of pickets. These included the special fleet of buses for the disabled for the safety of which the PTE was justifiably concerned. This contract had already been cancelled before the strike partly because of complaints that some of the hard-line drivers would give no assistance to the handicapped passengers. During February and March, temporary contracts were awarded to fill the gaps left by the withdrawal of Crosville. Merseybus, North Western and Shearing's of Wigan, were the principal beneficiaries.

Closure of Liverpool depot was a tragedy for Crosville as, with all the new contract work, it could have become a highly profitable operation. The management wanted to stay in Liverpool and many of the new employees, some of whom had known long periods of unemployment, desperately wanted to continue working. Management had a statutory duty to make the company saleable and could not do so in an anarchic environment.

More Town Lynx

The X5 (Murdishaw) and X7 (Chester) limited stop services to and from Liverpool had survived as commercial services. A second hourly Murdishaw route (X4), running hourly via Widnes, Cronton and the M62 proved popular then, in the spring of 1987, Crosville and North Western got together, combining Crosville X7 with North Western X37 to provide an hourly service (X8) between Chester, Ellesmere Port, Liverpool, Crosby, Southport and Banks, very closely resembling the controversial joint application of Crosville and Ribble in 1936, but much faster. The route required two Crosville and three North Western double-deck coaches and, as an introductory offer, purchase of a return ticket to Chester included the privilege of free travel on the Crosville local service to Chester Zoo and admission at a reduced

The immediate post-deregulation weeks found Crosville operating many unfamiliar routes gained under the Merseyside PTE tendering process. Daimler Fleetline HDG944 was one, of several of the type hired from the PTE and was still in PTE livery with Crosville fleet-names superimposed. It is seen alongside the Merseybus garage in Carisbrooke Road, Walton in November 1986.

rate. The Sunday service (X9) ran via the Zoo during the daytime but only between Liverpool and Banks in the evening.

At the same time, the two operators collaborated in a new service (X6) between Murdishaw, Widnes, Prescot, Old Swan, Liverpool, Aintree, M58 and Skelmersdale, hourly on weekdays (reduced in the evening), requiring two coaches of each operator. X6 and X8 connected at Skelhorne Street Bus Station and it was a commendable attempt at establishing a regional limited stop network. However, it did not last long; the Sunday X9 was withdrawn in January 1988, being resumed by North Western only in May and thereafter continuing as a seasonal service. In June, X6 was discontinued between Liverpool and Skelmersdale and Crosville withdrew from X8, North Western covering most of the missing journeys, but Crosville restarted an hourly Chester-Southport service X8 on 5th September, competing with North Western! The Murdishaw part lasted only another three months but was replaced by a new hourly X3 running between Murdishaw and Liverpool via Halebank, Menlove Avenue and Smithdown Road. X5 was doubled to half-hourly, combining with X3 and X4 to give four coaches an hour between Murdishaw, Runcorn and Liverpool, effectively capturing the through traffic from the local service H20-21, most journeys on which had been rerouted via Childwall Valley Road as H30-31 in February 1988. Further changes came in September 1989 when two journeys an hour on X5 were extended to Norton Priory on an increased 20-minute frequency and X3 was withdrawn.

Following a change of ownership (see below) joint working of X8/9 was resumed on 24th April 1989.

There were other positive developments in Liverpool. The contract for a link between the city centre and Albert Dock (222) using dedicated minibuses, running quarter-hourly from 10.0am to 8.0pm was won from 5th May 1988 and most of these trips were registered commercially for a time though it was given up in September 1989 and replaced by PMT (Red Rider). Another service (224) between Moorfields Station and Brunswick Business Park started under contract in November 1988 but this, too, was lost to Red Rider a year later. Meanwhile other operators were winning contracts on Crosville services; Warrington Transport ran the H5 on Sundays and a short-lived operator, Five Star Travel of Penketh won the Sunday service on H25, a trip on H21 and restarted the H2 through to Liverpool every 90 minutes, daytime only, commercially. This operator failed in mid-1989 and Crosville took over the operation including the commercial H2.

The Wirral Scene

The situation in Wirral in October 1986 closely resembled that in Liverpool. Most existing services were registered but few of them in the evenings and on Sundays. The former PTE 71A, Woodside-Heswall via Irby, was also registered as 71 and Merseybus did not register it. Crosville itself picked up most of the contracts for the evening and Sunday services and, in addition, secured some former PTE routes. On the debit side, Merseybus won the contracts for all three Birkenhead-Chester services on Sundays, C3 being curtailed to run between Hooton Station and Chester only. There was an hourly Chester-Liverpool service (C5) via the Birkenhead Tunnel and the all-day Heswall-Liverpool 419 was replaced by extensions of 72 to Liverpool, again via the Birkenhead Tunnel as 72A. At peak times, the 418 continued and was joined by a 417 via Irby. A few peak journeys ran through

Freight Rover Sherpa minibuses appeared in many different liveries as shown. From top to bottom –
MSR714 with 16-seat Dormobile body stands at West Kirby station on the Caldy local service on the first day of deregulation – 26th October 1986. It has not yet acquired a corporate livery being mainly plain white. Several of this batch went on hire to Merseybus whose minis had not arrived in time.

MSR777. again in West Kirby, bears the first Mini-Lynx livery with black leaping lynx.

MSR788 passes St.George's Hall, Liverpool on route 222 Albert Dock Circular on 3rd July 1989 with the second Mini-Lynx logo in lower case lettering.

After acquisition of Crosville by PMT there were many vehicle transfers between the company's divisions. Freight Rover Sherpa 413 is an original PMT vehicle with 20-seat body built by the operator. Mini-Lynx decals have been added together with a Crosville label in the windscreen.

Deregulation day, 26th October 1986 found Crosville buses on service at Seacombe ferry, a cherished goal never achieved in the 'twenties. Bristol VR DVL353 is working to New Brighton via Seabank Road on tendered service 101, a subsidised version of route 1 which originated as a frequent tram route in 1902 and was once the most profitable route on the erstwhile Wallasey Corporation system. The 'Merseytravel' card is not in evidence; possibly they had not all filtered through the system by the first day.

Leyland Olympian DOG104 turns out of Rycroft Road into Gorsedale Road in the Somerville district of Wallasey on 22nd January 1987. The route was designed for midibuses having been opened by Wallasey Corporation with an Albion Nimbus in 1962 and parked cars were a serious problem in narrow residential roads. The 'Merseytravel' card, indicating that it is a PTE subsidised service, can be seen in the nearside forward window. The route has changed hands several times and is usually worked by minibuses.

between Neston and Liverpool as 88B.

The Mold service was diverted to run as F11 between Ellesmere Port, Hooton and Mold, hourly during the day and early evening; on Sundays it ran to Hooton Station only. Operation was shared with Crosville Wales.

Gains by Crosville included the following:-

- 101 New Brighton-Seacombe-Park Station-Woodside (-hourly evenings & Sundays)
- 118-9 Mill Park-New Ferry or Spital-Prenton-Arrowe Park Hospital (hourly daily) extended via Upton, Ford Estate and Liscard to New Brighton on Sundays.
- 123-4 Somerville-Liscard-Leasowe Estate-Moreton Shore-Upton-Arrowe Park Hospital (hourly Mon. to Sat. daytime).
- 141 Woodside-Mill Park (½-hourly evenings and Sundays and some early morning trips)
- 147 Moreton Cross-Sandbrook Estate-Laird Street-Central Station (½-hourly daily)
- 151 Park Station-Charing Cross-Derby Road-Port Sunlight (½-hourly daily)
- 170 Woodside-Prenton Dell-Woodchurch Estate (½-hourly evenings and Sundays)

There were also contracts for mainly early morning trips on 133, 164-5, 168-9 and 190.

An innovation was a subsidised local service between West Kirby and Caldy (182) which ran along Croft Drive; this was eagerly acclaimed by the domestic workers but frowned upon by the owners of the highly-rated properties. It did not last long!

However, there were disquieting signs for the company as coach operators and some new entrepreneurs saw opportunities for expansion in the new regime. A.C. Parsons' Arrowebrook Coaches successfully tendered for the Sunday service on C22-23 Chester-West Kirby and an Ellesmere Port-Helsby trip on F54 from the first day of deregulation. Lofty's Tours of Bridge Trafford also gained contracts in Ellesmere Port and was destined to establish a thin network all over Wirral. Chester City ventured outside its boundary and took over Crosville work.

Competition

The more affluent districts of Wirral were fertile areas for minibus operation and a substantial order for 16-seat Freight Rover Sherpas had already been fulfilled before deregulation. They immediately appeared on routes between West Kirby, Caldy, Irby and Heswall. A subsidised minibus service (112) commenced between New Ferry and Poulton Lancelyn on 27th October 1986 and when the contract came up for renewal a year later, it was expanded into a network (112-4) covering much of residential Lower and Higher Bebington. Meanwhile, the Ellesmere Port town services, almost all subsidised by Cheshirebus, were converted to a new minibus network from February 1987 under the brand name Minilynx. Toppings' Super Coaches, trading as Toppline secured the Heswall-Banks Road local service on re-tendering in January 1987 and Avon Minis got the Arrowe Park Hospital-West Kirby evening and Sunday service (181) in March and a strange West Kirby-Greasby-Saughall Massie service in May. Worse still, PMT Ltd. of Stoke-on-Trent, originally one of the oldest BET subsidiaries, opened a depot in Pasture Road, Moreton and started tendering for services in both Wirral and Liverpool under the name Red Rider.

Many of the tendered services changed hands almost annually. The record for a mixture went to C22-23 which, by October 1989 sported five operators – Crosville, Crosville Wales, Arrowebrook, Matthews Coaches and Red Rider.

In one case Crosville seems to have been particularly predatory towards a new independent. On 4th January 1988, W.O. Blythin, t/a Busman Buses, started a commercial circular service B1-2 linking Woodside with Ford Estate, Upton, Arrowe Park Hospital and Woodchurch Road, using ex-PTE Daimler Fleetlines painted mainly white. Blythin also traded as Gold Star International of St. Asaph so perhaps Crosville had old scores to settle. On 28th March Crosville introduced a competing B1 and Merseybus a competing B2, Crosville using buses specially painted white to resemble Blythin's just as they had done in 1921 to J.M. Hudson in Ellesmere Port. In October Blythin got his own back by taking the contracts for 151 and 177 (Heswall via Storeton) from Crosville so, from the day these started, a B2 service was added by Crosville, followed a few months later by an additional circular by a slightly different route, B3-4. Blythin finally gave up and withdrew his service from 31st July 1989.

A new commercial Minilynx service C10 started on 4th September 1989 between Stanney Grange and New Brighton, competing with Merseybus service 10 between Rock Ferry and New Brighton and aping the original 10 which, at its full extent, had run between Bromborough and New Brighton. Merseybus replied two days later with 66 running between Clatterbridge, Bromborough and Stanney Grange with a maximum off-peak fare of 60p and special return fares in the Cheshire area whereupon Crosville doubled the service between Rock Ferry and New Brighton to every 15 minutes, full size buses being used on this section. Eventually, Merseybus withdrew their 66 but Crosville retained their C10 between New Brighton and Rock Ferry until February 1991. That year saw withdrawals by both companies, Crosville getting exclusive control of some ex-municipal routes such as 70/70A, Woodside-Woodchurch Estate, while the Merseybus presence in Chester was increased.

The Ellesmere Port network was frequently revised. From August 1987 the Clatterbridge hospital journeys (F58) were shared with Lofty's and in June 1988, three all day town services were lost to a Chester operator, Devaway. C.& M. Travel of Aintree secured a foothold in the town two months later. June 1988 also saw the loss of the Birkenhead-Parkgate service with the commercial extension

Ellesmere Port bus station on 9th June 1989 with Leyland Olympian DOG112 en route from Chester to Birkenhead and 1978 Leyland National SNL368 on a town service. The minibus behind the Olympian belongs to Devaway, one of the operators who made heavy inroads into Crosville local services in the post-deregulation years.

Crosville conducted a particularly predatory campaign against O. Blythin's Busman Buses circular services B1-2 in Birkenhead and painted Bristol VR DVL329 white to resemble Blythin's livery. In this view, taken in Greasby in March 1990, it has strayed on to route 37, an original Crosville route which the company has since abandoned, leaving Merseybus in possession.

It was not unusual for vehicles in the Town Lynx livery to be used on local services and Bristol VR DVL342 was caught by the camera in Upton village in June 1990 on the erstwhile route 83 between Woodside and West Kirby. The village has regained much of its secluded air since it was by-passed.

Heswall bus station on 6th August 1988 with 1979 Leyland Leopard ELL336 with 49-seat Duple body loading for West Kirby and Olympian DOG169 working the tortuous route through Thornton Hough, Clatterbridge and Bromborough to Eastham Ferry. ELL336 was originally classifed as a coach CLL336 but was equipped for service work and downgraded.

of Merseybus services 10-10A from Clatterbridge to Parkgate, giving a through service from New Brighton via Woodside. A new commercial C6 from Ellesmere Port via Port Sunlight, Higher Tranmere and Birkenhead to Liverpool, partly absorbing the tendered 151, was a failure and lasted just two months.

This was the nadir of Crosville in Wirral; the company's tendering was frequently not competitive and a rough analysis of contracts between March 1987 and January 1990 reveals 39 losses and only 20 gains.

New Owners

Crosville was one of the last NBC companies to be sold, the purchaser being ATL (Western) Ltd. of Rotherham, an associate of ATL Holdings, parent company of Carlton PSV (Sales) Ltd who had bought the business of National Travel (East) Ltd from the NBC in January 1987 and, prior to that, the private company, Yelloway Motor Services of Rochdale. The company, with 470 vehicles and 1,169 staff, went over to the new owners on 25th March 1988. Crosville Wales had been sold three months earlier to its management team and, coincidentally, it too had 470 vehicles. ATL was inexperienced in the bus business and soon ran into trouble, particularly with vehicle maintenance, and Yelloway's Operator's Licence was cancelled. This led to Crosville taking over some of that company's operations, working from a depot in Rochdale. However, ATL decided to get out of the bus business as quickly as possible and Crosville was again sold to the Drawlane Group on 18th February 1989.

Drawlane of Salisbury, was one of the initial success stories of deregulation, the other being the Stagecoach Group of Perth. North Western, which had taken over Ribble operations on Merseyside, was a Drawlane company and saw opportunities for rationalisation. The Hon. Richard Stanley joined the Drawlane board and was appointed chairman of Crosville; public statements predicted the return of the company to its former pre-eminent position. Most of the new entrepreneurs saw good pickings in the disposal of land and buildings which were not strictly essential to the operation and one of the first Crosville casualties was Heswall depot which closed on 4th September 1988, most of the fleet going to Rock Ferry though buses for routes C22/23, school contracts, and the minis went to West Kirby. The bus station remained in use until 10th April 1989, after which considerable nuisance and traffic congestion was caused by buses standing on the main Chester-West Kirby road while the station stood empty and barricaded. There was great public indignation and eventually the PTE and Wirral Borough Council financed the construction of a smaller station which opened on 2nd December 1990. West Kirby depot, too, was closed soon afterwards leaving only Rock Ferry operational. Drawlane also decided to close North Western's Skelhorne Street Bus Station which was also used by some Crosville limited stop services. This triggered the first stage of a rationalisation between Drawlane and Stagecoach in the north west.

Crosville-North Western Integration

From 11th September 1989, when Skelhorne Street Bus Station closed, a number of Crosville and North Western interurban services were linked across Liverpool to form the following through routes:-

300/302	Southport-Maghull-Liverpool-Cronton-Farnworth-Warrington
351	Ormskirk-Maghull-Crosby-Liverpool-Garston-Widnes-Runcorn
H30-31	Thornton-Crosby-Liverpool-Tarbock (H30) or Halebank (H31)-Runcorn Shopping City

The evening and Sunday services were still worked separately, terminating at Hood Street Gyratory or Mann Island. These link-ups solved some of the problems arising from Crosville no longer having a depot in Liverpool.

Crosville's Runcorn and Warrington operations were transferred to North Western from 25th September 1989; Northwich followed on 27th January 1990. Crewe services went to Drawlane subsidiary Midland Red North while other operations in Cheshire and at Rochdale went to Drawlane companies Bee Line and C-Line leaving Crosville only with Rock Ferry, Ellesmere Port and Chester depots and the operations from these centres, together with the name 'Crosville' were purchased by PMT Ltd of Stoke-on-Trent from 2nd February 1990. The Crosville company, still possessed of a number of assets including buses not required by the new owners, was renamed North British Bus Co. Ltd. from 30th March 1990.

The new Crosville fleet title and leaping lynx logo introduced in 1986

Bristol VR DVL421, in Town Lynx cream, red and green livery, waits to turn from Park Road North into Duke Street, Birkenhead on route C10, originally running between New Brighton and Ellesmere Port but later shortened to Rock Ferry. This route was part of the 'war' between Crosville and Merseybus in 1989-90.

Croft Drive East, Caldy is one of the best addresses in Wirral and never expected to have a bus service. Leyland Leopard ELL507 with 49-seat Duple body provides a standard of luxury in keeping with the neighbourhood when en route from West Kirby to Heswall on 14th September 1987.

One of 11 Leyland Lynx buses, new in 1990, No.854 was originally based at PMT's Burslem depot but had moved to Chester by 12th August 1991 when seen passing the closed Crosville West Kirby depot which was shortly to be demolished. It was in full PMT livery without a mention of Crosville.

From late 1990, Crosville buses in Wirral started appearing in PMT-style liveries. Despite several ex-Crosville buses being renumbered by dropping the prefix and adding 2000 or 3000 to the fleet number, eventually Crosville numbers were retained in full and applied in bold letters and numerals. Leyland Olympian DOG166 is seen passing the old Town Hall in Hamilton Square, Birkenhead in July 1991 in red and yellow livery with Crosville fleet name in PMT style. It is working route 72 to Heswall via Pensby.

PMT (Crosville) Dennis Darts with 35-seat PMT bodies were introduced at Rock Ferry depot in January 1992 for services 41/41A and 70/70A. They were given the Crosville-type prefix MDC though they were far from being 'minis'. MDC904 is seen loading at the new Woodside central loading island built in 1991.

CHAPTER 10
LONG DISTANCE SERVICES

Simultaneously with the development of local services, Crosville devoted some attention to running summer seasonal services to North Wales and other local attractions. A booking office was opened in Market Street, Hoylake and, from an early date, charabanc trips played an important part in the summer activities of West Kirby depot. In the early twenties, the charabanc with a row of doors along the nearside, a folding canvas hood and celluloid side screens for use in wet weather, was the normal vehicle to use for these activities.

By 1924, there were 14 charabancs (8 Leylands and 6 Daimlers) in the 127-strong Crosville fleet and the company had renumbered nine of them so that there was a continuous series from 8 to 21. They were used, according to availability, for all types of leisure service including the Singleton Avenue-Thurstaston and Moreton Cross-Shore trips, operated according to demand.

Before the 1930 Road Traffic Act came into force, there was no firm dividing line between the excursion run on demand and the regular timetabled express service and the regular North Wales coast services of local operators such as Wirral Motor Transport and Macdonald and Co. evolved from day excursions. Crosville's services, however, were established as regular services and they operated according to the published timetables irrespective of the number of bookings. A reputation for reliability was thus built up as people learned that there were no disappointments if a booking was made with Crosville. The company was at a disadvantage compared to the local charabanc operators as its summer routes were restricted to the same peripheral termini as its other services whereas Hardings and other operators were permitted to load at Woodside, though their standing time was strictly limited.

The potential for day-tripper traffic to North Wales had been demonstrated by the success of the New Ferry-Mold service started in 1923 and from 4th June 1924, a daily summer service was started from Singleton Avenue, Birkenhead to Mold, Loggerheads and Ruthin followed from 16th July by a similar facility commencing from Wallasey Village via Moreton, Hoylake and West Kirby. The times were co-ordinated from Heswall so that when traffic was light, only one bus needed to run through. In 1925 the Wallasey service had been extended back to commence at Liscard and both services reached Denbigh by 1926.

Because of high tolls on the Woodside vehicular ferry, the Liverpool operators rarely ran trips to North Wales as it was cheaper for the passengers to cross the river individually. From 8th July 1926, Crosville introduced a daily service from Liverpool (Canning Place) to Chester, Mold and Loggerheads, using the Widnes-Runcorn Transporter Bridge at a return fare of 5/-. Leaving Liverpool at 9.45am, it arrived at Chester at 12.10, Mold at 1.0 and Loggerheads at 1.15pm. There it met the Liscard and Birkenhead services to which transfer could be made for Ruthin and Denbigh. The bus was due back in Liverpool at 9.55pm. The trip was popular and licences were granted in Widnes for six buses for use on this service.

In 1927, Crosville bought the Tea House and part of the Loggerheads Estate and the following year there was an intensive campaign to popularise the place supported by combined bus and lunch or tea tickets available not only on the direct services but from places as far afield as Newcastle-under-Lyme and Crewe, by changing at Chester. In 1928 afternoon journeys were being run from both Liscard and Singleton Avenue, allowing 1 -2 hours stay. These were run with charabancs and were not co-ordinated from Heswall.

Coastal Routes

Co-ordinated services from Liscard and Singleton Avenue to Prestatyn and Rhyl were advertised to start on 19th May 1926 but were delayed until June because of the after-effects of the General Strike which delayed the delivery of new buses. In 1928, the service was altered to start at Park Station instead of Singleton Avenue, running thence via Upton and Pensby to Heswall where it still made connection with the Liscard bus running via West Kirby. In the same year, a daily Park Station-West Kirby-Llandudno service, giving five hours stay in the resort started on 16th May. This ran via Mold, Afonwen, the Vale of Clwyd and St. Asaph. A further service, introduced in 1929, operated between Park Station and Llanrwst via West Kirby, Chester, Llangollen, Corwen and Betws-y-Coed.

Park Station was a better prospect than Singleton Avenue as it was connected directly to Liverpool by the Mersey Railway and was the next best thing to Woodside ferry. The summer services were very successful, providing valuable new leisure facilities for Merseyside people and a standard of reliability which the excursion operators could not equal. They also established a firm foundation for future developments.

London and the Midlands

The coach services between Merseyside and London were highly competitive and at one time there were seven

This chain-driven Lacre charabanc (FM 535 - no fleet number has been traced), bore the name Grey Knight. The vehicle lasted well into the 'twenties and was fitted with pneumatic tyres on the front wheels as shown. Note the oil lamps and the logo on each door.

operators running on various versions of the route but mainly via Stratford-on-Avon and Oxford. Imperial of Liverpool and Rymer's Ideal had started the first services in May 1928 and in August and September of that year Crosville experimented with some weekend excursions from Birkenhead (Woodside) though how permission to use this terminus was obtained is not known. These trips departed on Fridays and returned on Mondays and one could book for a weekend or for 10 days. The results were sufficiently encouraging for the company to start a daily service from Birkenhead Park Station on 28th March 1929, picking up at West Kirby, Heswall, Chester and Crewe; this followed the Stratford and Oxford route. A second service starting at Liverpool Pier Head and calling at Widnes, Warrington, Sandbach and Crewe, started on 16th May 1929, running via Coventry and St. Albans. The Liverpool service was suspended for the winter but the Birkenhead service continued. Fares had stabilised at 15/- single and £1.7.6d return but during the winter there was a rate cutting war and from 6th November 1929, Crosville's Birkenhead-London fare was 12/- single, £1 return.

Various detail changes were made to the London services but for the 1930-31 winter one service ran, starting in Liverpool and crossing to Birkenhead by ferry. Licensing restrictions when the 1930 Act came into force and acquisitions gradually eliminated the competition until, with the purchase of Pearsons' business in May 1935, Crosville became the sole operator. Surprisingly, in view of the fuel restrictions, a limited wartime service was permitted from 24th September 1939 but all such services were withdrawn by September 1942.

Birmingham had very strict licensing laws so most of the London services could not enter the city, calling, instead at Erdington on the north-eastern outskirts. A Birkenhead-Birmingham service with 9.0am and 4.0pm departures from Woodside was started by Crosville on 28th May 1930 so must have been planned during the period of LMS ownership, perhaps with a view to abstracting the Great Western Railway's traffic as it travelled via Whitchurch and Shrewsbury. It ran for two seasons and was withdrawn on 27th September 1931, by agreement with the railways. Similarly a route from Newcastle-under-Lyme, (where Crosville had a small depot on the outskirts of the Potteries), via Crewe and Chester to Birkenhead started in June 1930 with one return journey per day; later there were two trips which kept one bus busy all day. This service, also, was withdrawn in September 1931.

The Caernarfon Services

A significant part of the 1930 Agreement with Birkenhead Corporation was a liberal policy by the Watch Committee in the matter of the grant of licences for long distance services and some of the results can be seen above. However, the most important services to be developed were those between Birkenhead and Caernarfon. UNU Motors of Llangefni, a business owned by Webster Bros. of Wigan

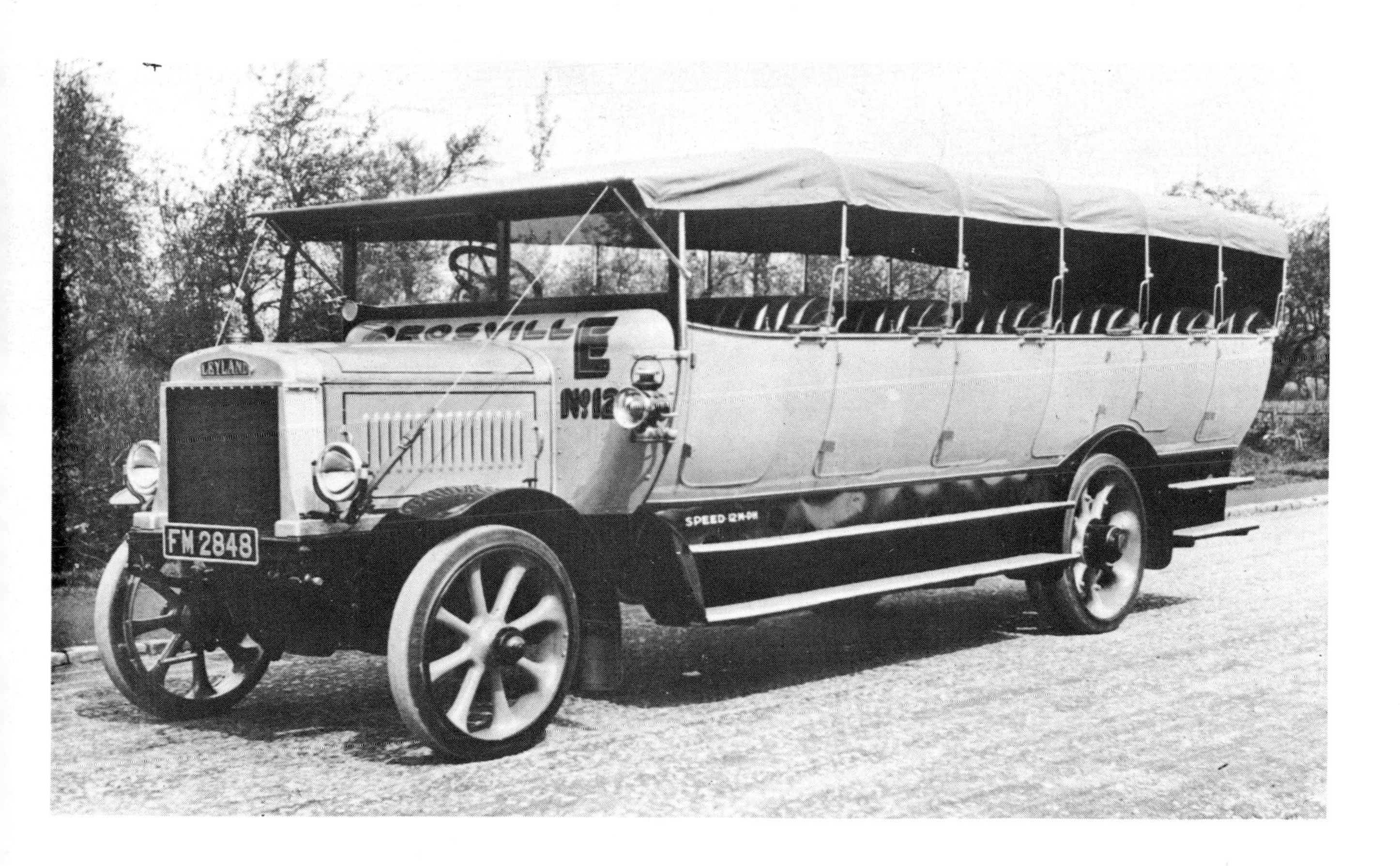

Charabancs were popular for recreational travel not just for excursions to North Wales but for comparatively short services such as Moreton Cross to the Shore and Singleton Avenue, Birkenhead to Thurstaston. No.12 was one of four 36 hp Leyland GH7s with Leyland coachwork placed in service in 1924 and numbered 12-15, (chassis No. 12793-6) though the second of the batch carried 'AC' instead of 13, to overcome superstition. The 28 seats were arranged in banks and extended right across the body, each row having its separate door on the nearside. Technical development was so rapid that all four were withdrawn and sold in 1928, probably being converted to lorries.

had been bought by the LMS Railway and merged with Crosville from 1st January 1930. During the 1929 season they had run a daily Caernarfon-Birkenhead service leaving at 8.45am and returning from Woodside at 6.0pm at 8/- single or 10/- return. The vehicles had been refused licences in Birkenhead so only return ticket holders could be picked up. Crosville started running on 4th June with 9.0am and 6.0pm departures from both ends and using the coastal route. From December 1930 the North Wales services were reorganised so as to establish a comprehensive network before the cut-off date for new services under the 1930 Act on 9th February 1931.

The Caernarfon service now started at Liverpool using the Woodside ferry and was split into two routes, the coastal route (Service A) and an inland service (B) via Chester, Wrexham. Llangollen, Betws-y-Coed and Capel Curig. For the 1931 season, the remaining Singleton Avenue services were withdrawn, the Denbigh service being diverted to Woodside via Eastham. The Llandudno-Park Station service had previously been extended to commence at Seacombe Ferry, calling at Egremont and Liscard and the Llanrwst service ran to Woodside via Park Station but was finally merged in the Caernarfon 'B' service in 1936.

During the formative period, there was fierce competition from Macdonald & Co. (Maxways) and Wirral Motor Transport Co., both of which were acquired by Crosville in 1934. Pearsons' Happy Days and All-British Line also ran on the route but failed to obtain licences under the 1930 Act. From 25th May 1936 there were 10 journeys per day between Liverpool and Caernarfon, four via Holywell and St. Asaph, four via Flint and Rhyl and two via Llangollen. The winter service was approximately half of this and the pattern remained the same until the 1939 summer season was brought to a premature end by the outbreak of war.

There was considerable community of interest between Wirral and North Wales and the Crosville services made a strong contribution not only to the growth of tourism but to social exchanges. Through tickets to virtually every village in Caernarfonshire and Anglesey established confidence in the service and built up a valuable all-the-year-round clientele.

Post-War Express

The first long distance service to be reinstated after the war was the Liverpool-Caernarfon B service via Wrexham, Llangollen and Betws-y-coed, priority being given to this route because of the relative inaccessibility of the places en route and the poor train service. It recommenced on 1st December 1945 with one daily return journey worked from the Caernarfon end. The Caernarfon coastal services and the Liverpool-London day and night services restarted on 1st April 1946 together with the Monday to Friday Wrexham-

1931 — 1st Winter Issue

LIVERPOOL

BIRKENHEAD—WARRINGTON—
WALLASEY—CHESTER—CREWE
AND POTTERIES

TO

LONDON

BY THE FAMOUS "TIGER" SALOON COACH SERVICES

WEEKDAYS AND SUNDAYS

Route CC1/333

LIVERPOOL—LONDON (Euston)

Via LICHFIELD—STRATFORD-ON-AVON—OXFORD

Route CC1/338

LIVERPOOL—LONDON (Victoria)

Via LICHFIELD—COVENTRY—NORTHAMPTON

A journey between Liverpool and London by road cannot be undertaken with greater comfort, reliability and security than is provided by Crosville Motor Services Ltd., whose extensive organisation ensures that the finest Services are maintained and the interests of passengers safeguarded in every way.

IT'S THE SERVICE THAT MATTERS.

Proprietors: CROSVILLE MOTOR SERVICES LTD., Crane Wharf, Chester.

20,000—10/31—1 S. 5,000—G.R.G. Ltd.

For several years Crosville time-table leaflets sported broadside views of vehicles and this 1931 folder shows 1930 Leyland Tiger 370, one of six (369-74, later K27-32) dedicated to the Liverpool-London services, which had standard Leyland bus bodies adapted for long distance operation. Note the two doors, opening outwards and the inward facing seats over the rear axle. The service via Coventry and Northampton had just been acquired from the Merseyside Touring Co., by then a Ribble subsidiary. It was transferred to Crosville under the BAT Area Agreement scheme but was withdrawn following duplication restrictions imposed under the new road service licensing laws.

These pictures (below and below right) span 22 years and typify a Crosville renaissance. Leyland Tiger TS4 742 was new in 1933 being dedicated to the Liverpool-Caernarfon services as indicated by the illuminated panels at roof level and the legend on the glass window louvres – 'Birkenhead-Abergele-Llandudno-Bangor-Caernarvon' (sic). Unusually, the 32-seat body was by Leyland who normally showed little interest in luxury coach bodies. It became K69. In the post-war period it was one of a number of vehicles rebodied with a standard Eastern Coach Works body as fitted to the L type; a diesel engine and Covrad radiator was fitted and it was renumbered KA190. It was photographed at Heswall in October 1955.

This 1936 Leyland Tiger TS7 was one of 12 with Harrington body which typified the style of the coaches used on the Liverpool-Caernarfon services in the late 'thirties. The basic body colour was light grey with green relief and black mudguards and beading. Half of the batch, including K103, had 33 seats but six had only 25 seats in a 2+1 configuration. All were reseated in 1948 to 32 or 33 seats and five of the 12 received diesel engines and new KA fleet numbers. The lower picture shows KA210, formerly K100, at Liverpool Pier Head on the weekend Amlwch service. The Harrington body did not adapt well to the post-war cream and green livery.

The four original 1929 Leyland Tiger TS2 London coaches (or 'buses-de-luxe' as the company described them at the time), Nos.175-8, had ordinary Leyland bus bodies with coach seats and outward-opening hinged doors. They were downgraded to the Birkenhead-Caernarfon service the following year and eventually painted in the grey and green coach livery. They became K17-20 in the 1935 renumbering and after rebodying, continued in service until the 'fifties.

Birkenhead express which resumed at its pre-war fare of 2/6d single or return, though this was increased to 3/- in 1947. Most of the seasonal North Wales services resumed operation in the summer of 1946.

There was a tremendous demand for these facilities and vehicle shortages and fuel rationing restricted facilities in the first post-war season, advance booking being strictly enforced. The pre-war system of connections for other destinations at Bangor and Caernarfon was too unwieldy to handle the numbers involved and, for the 1947 summer season, new services through from Liverpool to Porthmadog, Criccieth and Pwllheli and to Amlwch were provided at weekends. The new Butlin's Holiday Camp near Pwllheli provided an enormous volume of new traffic. The Amlwch service, which ran on Fridays, Saturdays, Sundays and Mondays was soon extended to Cemaes Bay.

A nine day wonder in 1945 was Crosville's investigation of the practicability of using adapted military amphibious vehicles (DUKWs – usually known as 'ducks') for public service. A Dee crossing was seen as an attractive proposition in view of the potential saving in time and mileage between Merseyside and North Wales. There were plenty of amphibians for sale and vague plans were drawn up for services between Wirral and Rhyl, Colwyn Bay and Llandudno. However, experiments on a piece of water near Warrington soon made it clear than unless the water was dead calm and there were no hazards, such transport was unsafe.

In 1951, MacShanes applied for a competitive Liverpool-London service on the grounds that the Crosville service was unable to satisfy the exceptional demand generated by the Festival of Britain at the South Bank; this was refused but Crosville was granted unlimited duplication for the period of the Festival. This was not entirely utilised as hundreds of disappointed would-be passengers were booked at Ribble's Liverpool office to travel on the Warrington-London service operated by Scout Motor Services and the Ribble subsidiary, W.C. Standerwick, the connecting link being provided by Crosville!

During the fifties there was a demand for new long distance facilities, most of which were vigorously opposed by the railways. An application by Crosville and Midland Red for a joint service between Liverpool and Leicester via Wolverhampton, Birmingham and Coventry took eight days before the Traffic Commissioners, 81 public witnesses being called in support, but it still failed. More successful were new summer Saturday services between Widnes and Pwllheli (Butlins) which started on 22nd May 1954 and Liverpool and Aberystwyth from 2nd July 1955.

People in the new residential districts were demanding direct facilities for holiday travel and Huyton, Speke, Hale, Upton, Greasby and Ellesmere Port were given summer weekend facilities to the North Wales coast. More suburban picking-up points were also added on the London services.

The opening of the new Conwy bridge on 14th December 1958 enabled double-deck buses to reach Conwy, Bangor and Caernarfon by the coastal route and special Lodekka coaches were provided to enable duplication to be cut

Originally a 25-seat luxury coach allocated to the Liverpool-London service and new in 1934 as 965, Leyland Tiger TS6 K85 with Duple body is shown at the Pier Head in February 1949 after being reseated to 32 and repainted green and cream. The upper panels originally carried an illuminated legend 'Crosville Liverpool-London Express'. It retained a petrol engine until withdrawn in 1952.

down. Changes in social habits virtually eliminated the demand for daily operation of the relatively short North Wales expresses such as Wallasey-Llandudno upon which the network had been based in the late twenties and early 'thirties. In the early sixties, mid-week day returns at weekend single fare were offered on the Liverpool-Caernarfon services over certain sections between Liverpool and Llandudno and these were extended to all stages in 1965.

In the Spring of 1960 the London coaches started to use the then uncompleted M1 Motorway and from 1963 the London night service was run daily throughout the year; in recent years it had run only at weekends in the winter. As the motorway network was extended, there were frequent changes and a dramatic acceleration of the London services to little more than a third of the pre-war 12 hour running time. A special Friday facility (X18) at 4.30pm from London to Liverpool via M1, M6 and Birkenhead, running northbound only was introduced in March 1968 and made it possible for workers in London to spend a long weekend on Merseyside, the return trip being made on the Sunday night service. In 1973 a Chester-Caernarfon connection (L18) was added.

The run-down of railway services in the Beeching era opened the way for new long distance services. Liverpool-Cardiff (X71), jointly operated with Western Welsh, and based on the ex-Mid-Wales Motorways Newtown-Cardiff service, started running daily on 26th July 1964, continuing at weekends during the winter. This improved access to the delightful scenery of central Wales which had been largely remote from the express service network. A Friday night service through to Barry Island was added in 1966.

A new kind of winter express service, designed to link various places to Liverpool or Manchester on one or two days per week also emerged during the sixties. More on the lines of an excursion but without the restrictive conditions as to catchment area and day return fare conditions, these originated in small Welsh towns such as Llanidloes to Liverpool (X74-Thursdays) or Manchester (X75-Saturdays) which commenced in September 1964. An Ellesmere Port-Manchester service (X16), through Frodsham and Runcorn on Thursdays and Saturdays, which commenced in February 1967 also acted as a feeder to the X61 London service at Runcorn. It was extended to start from Little Sutton and again, in 1970, from Bromborough though the Thursday journey was dropped.

The 1967 season saw new joint ventures with Lancashire United, North Western and Trent for Saturday services from Liverpool to Skegness and to Nottingham. Ellesmere Port-Skegness and Scarborough services were unsuccessful and were not continued. In 1971, Crosville and Home James Coaches combined their competing North Wales summer services into a joint Huyton-Llandudno service (X9).

From 1974, the National Express network took over and although Crosville coaches were, to a large extent, still used, their identity was lost under the bland all-white corporate livery.

The 1930 Leyland Tiger coaches for the Liverpool-London services originally carried Leyland bus bodies with superior seating. This coach was originally No.374 of this batch and was rebodied in by Eastern Coach Works in 1939 with a style of bodywork used for both buses and coaches. In its post-war green and cream livery it was classified as a dual-purpose vehicle and retained its petrol engine until withdrawn in 1952.

Leyland Tiger TS7 (K109) with Burlingham body in the grey and green livery of the 'thirties was an odd coach having been ordered by the Llanrug, Caernarfon, operator D.M. Prichard before take-over in 1936. In 1948 it was fitted with a Leyland diesel engine, becoming KA183, and in the following year its body was extensively rebuilt by the maker. After withdrawal in 1957 it saw further service for the well-known contractor, Sir Alfred McAlpine, at Ellesmere Port.

New in 1932 as 643 and later K66, this Leyland Tiger TS2 had a chequered career having been sold to the military in 1941, bought back in 1947, and fitted with a Burlingham coach body, Covrad radiator and diesel engine, being renumbered KA203. Note that 'Crosville' has been cast into the radiator header tank, a practice adopted by several large companies. It was photographed at the Pier Head on a Caernarfon working on 9th October 1950 and was to work for another three seasons.

The shortage of coaches in the immediate post-war years condemned many passengers to make quite lengthy journeys in service buses and KW277, a Bristol LL6B 35-seat bus, new in 1952, is shown en route for Llandudno Junction. Doubtless the rear seats are piled with luggage.

Variations in body detail are demonstrated by 1952 Bristol LS6G CUG296 (formerly UG296) with curved corner windows and similar LS6B UW328 (later CUB328) of 1953 with divided windscreen. These 39-seat coaches incorporated the black relief round the windows which improved the appearance of the all cream coaches. Both vehicles were fitted with bus type indicators and jack-knife doors in 1960-61. In 1967 they were converted for one-man operation, the installation of a luggage pen reducing the seating by two. They were both scrapped, still classified as a coaches, in 1970.

The first batch of eight Bristol Lodekka double-deck coaches entered service between Liverpool and Llandudno in 1954, the restricted dimensions of the old Conwy bridge preventing their use further west. The low centre of gravity of the Lodekka made it very acceptable as a coach. There were 22 seats and two luggage pens in the lower saloon and 30 seats on the upper deck which was reached by a straight staircase. The body design differed slightly from that of the standard Lodekka; there was a single window on the rear platform, off-side emergency door and curved off-side cab windows. By 1958 these vehicles had been fitted with three-piece front destination indicators and painted in dual-purpose green and cream livery. They were originally numbered ML675-82 and became DLB675-82 in 1958. They were eventually reseated to 31/24 and classified as buses from 1968. ML678 is seen at the Pier Head in 1955; ML680 at Rhyl in 1954 and ML681 on the Wallasey-Llandudno service near Bodelwyddan.

'Queen Mary' KW231 (later CLB231) a Bristol LL6B with superbly comfortable 35-seat Eastern Coach Works body was photographed at St. George's Plateau, Liverpool on 22nd May 1951, two months after entering service on the London run, with a similar coach behind. Note the white steering column and wheel. This coach ran for Crosville until 1964, seeing further service as a contractor's bus.

After the new Conwy Bridge was opened in December 1958, Crosville was able to run double-deck buses to points east of Llandudno Junction and these attractive 55-seat Bristol Lodekka coaches were placed on the Liverpool-Caernarfon service in December 1962. DFB113 was the last of five such vehicles which were repainted green and cream in 1968. The upper view shows it leaving Ribble's Skelhorne Street coach station in February 1963 while the lower view shows DFB111 at the Pier Head over 10 years later. The large luggage compartment, restricting the lower deck capacity to 18 is clearly visible in the lower picture. These buses were occasionally used on local service.

Crosville was the only operator to use the Widnes-Runcorn transporter bridge on service, a practice dating from 1926. A new LD6B Lodekka service bus (ML935) has been used on this Saturday service between Liverpool's south-eastern suburbs and Llandudno on 23rd August 1958.

A Bristol MWS6G (CMG) and an RELH6G (CRG) preparing to leave London, Victoria Coach Station on the overnight departure for Liverpool on 2nd May 1964. Note the illuminated route signs on the RE.

Crosville, like many other large operators, acquired lightweight coaches for private hire work. Bedford VAM70 CVF693 with a Duple 45-seat body entered service in June 1969. It was sold to a dealer in 1980 and later went to Eire.

With St. George's Hall and a flyover in the background, Bristol RELH6L coach CRL306 is seen en route to London in National Express white livery. The coach was one of nine with 47-seat Eastern Coach Works bodies which came into service in 1974.

CHAPTER 11
THE FLEET

Apart from a few second-hand vehicles and a handful of Lacres, the wartime fleet comprised Daimler CBs and CKs and 38 Daimler CKs were purchased during the post-war expansion period of 1919-20. There were also a few ex-RAF Crossleys which were used mainly for 'chasing' on competitive routes. Two Leyland G7s were added to the fleet in 1921 and from 1922, the company standardised on Leyland chassis and bought nothing else new for seven years. The 36 hp 4-cylinder G7 and its successors, the GH7, SG9 and SG11 were the standard models in 1923-25, though some smaller A7, A9 and A13 vehicles were also acquired. Leyland bodywork was preferred and the bodybuilder paid the company the compliment of naming a particular full-width cab design as the 'Crosville'. However, the half-cab type was gaining universal favour, not only for driver visibility but also access to the engine. Solid tyres were standard until 1924-25 after which technical progress produced pneumatic tyres suitable for heavy vehicles. Crosville built up traffic on new routes with the A type buses and changed over to the larger types as demand increased.

When Pye's business was acquired in 1924, an assortment of 13 buses, 6 charabancs and a lorry came into Crosville's possession; there were five Straker Squires, five Albions, two Pagefields, a Fiat, a Bristol, a Tilling Stevens, two Fords, a Dodge and a GMC. They were run only until new vehicles could be obtained.

The early Leylands were basically lorry chassis with straight chassis members, resulting in a very high body but in 1926 the first model with a chassis raised over the rear axle, the Lion PLSC1 with provision for 31 or 32 seats, was placed on the market and found immediate favour with the bus operators. The design was the half-way stage between the old high chassis and the later low level models which became accepted as normal by the end of the decade. A slightly longer model, the PLSC3, capable of carrying 35-36 seated passengers was soon added. A double-deck version, the LG1 Leviathan, was also available and Crosville bought 12 of these, specifically for the West Kirby-Park Station, West Kirby-Liscard and New Ferry-Bromborough services. Birkenhead Corporation, too, was a Leviathan user and 40 of the total output of 93 ran in Wirral.

In 1928, the 6-cylinder Leyland Titan TD1 lowbridge double-deck bus with an overall height just exceeding 13ft hit the market and changed the whole concept of double-deck bus operation. This type, with its 48-51 seat capacity, could now be considered for short-distance rural services where the passenger demand justified the extra capacity. The 3- and 4-seat benches upstairs and the sunken side gangway were far less of a hindrance to this type of operation than on urban service for which, nevertheless, they were extensively used. The original Titans had open staircases but a fully enclosed model was introduced in time for the Commercial Motor Show in 1929, the bus displayed being Crosville 367 (later L61) with 'LMS Crosville' oval fleet titles. Twelve of the open-staircase models were already in Crosville service in Wirral followed by 28 enclosed models in 1930. Another was acquired with Brookes Bros' White Rose business at Rhyl which also contributed six open-top Leviathans. All the open-staircase buses had been rebuilt with enclosed platforms by 1936.

Meanwhile, single-deck bus design forged ahead, the PLSC model being succeeded in the Crosville fleet in 1929 by the much lower 4-cylinder Lion LT1 and the 6-cylinder Tiger TS2 models. Although the latter was a better performer, in the early 'thirties, the company reserved the Tiger for long-distance work, fuel economy being, as ever, of prime importance. The LT and TS series were progressively improved throughout the 'thirties and many examples of both types were to be found in Crosville service. From 1936, as diesel engines became more numerous, the Tiger TS7 and TS8 models became the standard full-size single-decker.

In pre-war days Crosville was essentially a single-deck company, double-deckers being mainly confined to Merseyside and Crewe. Small numbers were based at Chester and Rhyl and there were two at Caernarfon for the Llanberis service. By 1939 they numbered 153, about 15% of the fleet. At the other end of the spectrum, there were 166 small, lightweight single-deckers seating between 20 and 30, most of which were Leyland Cubs, the first example of which entered the fleet in 1931. After the Road Traffic Act 1930 came into force, one-man operation was restricted to 20-seaters so there were numerous examples of this capacity as well as some 26-seaters. A half-cab 30-seater was developed to beat the weight restriction on Menai Bridge. The Cub was ideal for lightly-trafficked rural routes and for narrow lanes with tight turns; even Wirral with its relatively heavy traffic had a use for them and they could usually be found on the Birkenhead-Chester via Stanney and Stoak, Heswall via Storeton, Banks Road local and New Ferry-Moreton routes.

Double-deck Policy

After the all-Leyland Titan TD1 became available it became Crosville's policy to purchase only lowbridge double-deck vehicles so that they were fully interchangeable between depots. In pre-war days the only exception to this rule was the side-engined AEC 'Q' demonstrator AMD 256 which

Crosville's first No. 27 was one of four AEC YC types placed in service in 1919 and withdrawn when Leyland standardisation set in in 1923. The body is believed to have been built by Bartle.

This Daimler charabanc, bodied by Davidson of Trafford Park, is recorded as dating from 1916. It is probably one of three, Nos. 14-16, which were disposed of in 1919.

entered service on loan but in Crosville colours on the Liverpool-Mossley Hill-Garston route on 10th April 1933. The ultra-modern appearance of this vehicle contrasted so strongly with the old fashioned municipal buses and trams that this bus was quickly purchased for its publicity value even though it was completely non-standard. When the route was returned to Liverpool Corporation in 1938, the Q was transferred to Rock Ferry from where it usually worked on the Birkenhead-Chester group of routes until disposal in 1945.

As the Titan range was up-dated throughout the 'thirties, the Merseyside depots received allocations of each new batch, the V-fronted Leyland-bodied TD3s of 1934 and the more graceful Eastern Counties bodied TD4s of 1935 and 1936. The TD5s, delivery of which was spread over 1938-40, had bodies by Eastern Coach Works with two destination apertures at the front (though only the upper one was used on Merseyside) and one at the rear. This class reintroduced destination blinds to the company and the older double-deckers and the KA class of single-deck buses were also equipped though the older single-deckers continued to use Widd plates exclusively. Some displays were extremely cryptic e.g. 'E.PORT B'HEAD' for Birkenhead via Ellesmere Port. No provision was made for the Woodside-Ellesmere Port via Pooltown Road service so Widd plates bearing the letter 'P', similar to the alphabetical plates used in Liverpool, were also displayed.

Fleet Numbering

Crosville originally adopted a straightforward progressive numbering system except that some superstitious official decided that 13 should be replaced by 'AC', a stratagem applied to two successive vehicles. They were notorious gap-fillers and seemingly could not bear any gaps in the series, higher numbered vehicles being renumbered to fill the spaces. By 1934, 755 vehicles were numbered between 1 and 992 (plus 1000, the AEC 'Q' double-decker). A system was then devised consisting of an initial letter, denoting the vehicle type, with numbers starting at 1 in each series. Later, in some cases, a second letter was added to indicate what type of engine was fitted. This system lasted until 1958. An unusual event was the changeover from FM

Despite the vagaries of the British climate, the open motor coach was popular with the public and it took some years before the all-weather coach with sunshine roof became fully established. These short-length Leyland Lion PLSC1s demonstrate a midway point in design with a fixed roof at the front end and side windows. Number 267 demonstrates the open position (but without the metal frame which supported the canvas hood) while No. 268 is fully covered. The rear 'peep-holes' were of celluloid. This pair was not rebodied; they became A32-33 and were withdrawn in 1938. Crosville Motor Services Ltd.

This view of 1925 Leyland Leviathan 218 in the bright red livery, passing King's Gap, Hoylake on the West Kirby-Liscard service epitomises the urbanisation of the smaller Wirral towns of which Crosville was a catalyst in the 'twenties.

The Leyland Titan TD1 lowbridge double-decker was one of the most successful models ever built. The Leyland body was exactly 13ft high - 2-3 ft lower than contemporary types such as the Leviathan - and could be used on many rural routes hitherto limited to single-deckers. The upper deck seats were arranged in rows of three or four with a sunken off-side gangway on which unwary lower deck passengers could bump their heads when rising. The earlier models had open platforms and staircases and No. 325 was the first of Crosville's initial order for 12, delivered in May 1928. It is seen in the short-lived bright red livery and ran initially in Wirral but later migrated to Caernarfon for use on the Llanberis service. It had its rear end enclosed in the early 'thirties - all had been done by 1936 - and became L39 in the 1935 renumbering. It was used in regular service until 1952, being one of the last petrol-engined double-deckers in the fleet. Note the absence of a side lifeguard, a legal requirement after the passing of the Road Traffic Act, 1930.

Bristol K6B MW362 (Later DLB362) stands on Woodside ferry approach when new in 1949. It has yet to be equipped with destination blinds and displays a Widd plate in the front bulkhead window. The bus behind is a second-hand Craven bodied Leyland TD4 ex-Sheffield Corporation.

to AFM which occurred in the middle of a batch of Leyland Cubs, N105 being FM 9999 and N106 AFM 1. Years later, history repeated itself when a Leyland National was registered AFM 1W. The gap-filling policy continued within the new system and many vehicles bore three fleet numbers during their Crosville service.

Wartime Needs

Within months of the outbreak of war and the suspension of many services, Crosville found that increased employment, movement of service personnel and petrol rationing for private motorists were creating a need for a bigger rather than a smaller fleet. The September 1939 figure of 995 had increased to 1,101 (10.7%) by April 1940. At the time, there were plenty of operators with spare vehicles and the Regional Transport Commissioner arranged hiring between operators as necessary. Nobody hired their best buses and the need to maintain a larger, elderly fleet placed a great strain on the company's depleted maintenance facilities as many experienced, skilled men had left for the forces. Ten Birkenhead Corporation Titan TD1s were hired for a time but their owner soon needed them back. About 25% of Wallasey's fleet was surplus to requirements and, after helping out on rail replacement services in Liverpool, some worked on Crosville's Liverpool services until August 1941 when seven, mainly AEC Regents, were returned and the others were transferred to Wrexham where most remained until 1946. Some PLSC Lions were bought from Ribble, running from Rock Ferry in Ribble colours with Crosville transfers. Four of them were third-hand and, in 1943, five were fitted with new 34-seat Burlingham bodies to wartime utility specifications. The Cubs were an embarrassment; about 12 were sold and one was exchanged with the Thames Valley Traction Co. Ltd. for an elderly (but larger capacity) Leyland Tiger.

Crosville's desperate need was for double-deck buses and in 1940 the situation was eased by the completion of their own TD5 order (12 buses) and the diversion of 10 TD7s from East Kent and 16 from Southdown. The latter had highbridge bodies and most worked in Wirral, based at Rock Ferry and Chester. They were instantly recognisable by their GCD (Brighton) registration numbers. Manchester Corporation provided a number of TD1s and, after helping out in Liverpool in the post-blitz period, they were dispersed. One would occasionally be seen in Birkenhead having worked in from Mold, a route which had been converted to double-deck operation during the war.

Ten more 'unfrozen' Leyland TD7s, released by the government under wartime controls, joined the fleet in 1942, followed by 10 Guy Arabs with utility bodies, some with wooden seats. These Guys, and a further 11 in 1943, were allocated to Crewe but they released Leylands for service elsewhere. The only utility buses to see service in Merseyside were 22 Bristol K6As delivered in 1945-46 and mostly allocated to Liverpool. The first four had wooden seats but the remainder were built to the 'relaxed' specification with more opening windows and upholstered seating.

Second Hand Buses

In 1944-45, with 130 hired vehicles in the fleet, Crosville realised that it was very exposed as, with the end of the war in sight, most of the owners would want them back. They correctly foresaw that the increased demand would not cease with the end of hostilities so an approach was made to the owners with a view to purchasing the hired double-deckers. Initially, only 13 buses were acquired in this way but the search continued and by 1946, 65 buses, many of which were already 17 years old, had been purchased. There followed a remarkable period in the company's history when many of these veterans were fitted with diesel engines, rebodied and equipped with Tilling-style indicators. Many bodies were extensively rebuilt or exchanged between vehicles. The acquisition of second-hand vehicles continued

Leyland Lion LT5 No. 751 (later F4) introduced a transitional style of body by Eastern Counties. New in 1932, there were 42 vehicles in the class though some were bodied by Leyland. Most continued in service with petrol engines until 1950 or later.

Three Leyland Titan TD3s, new in 1933, were fitted with these stylish Eastern Counties lowbridge bodies. New as 934-6, they were renumbered M10-12 and, after rebodying by Eastern Counties in 1949, continued in service until 1955-56.

In 1939, a number of vehicles were rebodied by Eastern Coach Works of which 1932 Leyland Tiger TS4 No. K12 was an example. The same body shell was used for both service buses and coaches, the latter having superior interior trim and seating and sporting the grey and green livery and rather short-lived winged fleet name. Coach K12 ran until 1952 and was one of the last petrol-engined vehicles in the fleet.

until 1953. Perhaps the greatest achievement of Crosville's innovative engineering department was bus M639 which was built from the chassis frame of Birkenhead Corporation 205 (a 1935 Titan), running units from Crosville KA80 (a 1937 Leyland Tiger TS7) and a Salford Corporation body!

Most of the acquisitions were Leylands, though there were a few AECs but Tilling Group policy required a changeover to Bristol chassis for new vehicles in the post-war years. In this respect, the 1945 utility buses were a foretaste of things to come and in 1946 the first Bristol K6 double-deck and L6 single-deck buses with standard Eastern Coach Works bodies took to the streets in both Liverpool and Wirral. The most prominent features were the large Tilling-style destination and route indicators with a long destination box and a combined 'via' and route number screen. On the early models there were three sets of this equipment – front, rear and nearside over the door of the double-deckers. Many of the blinds were too long and would not turn and Crosville's lack of enthusiasm and somewhat amateurish allocation of route numbers clearly indicated that the company was complying reluctantly with a Group directive.

Tilling Group Style

The K type double-deckers of orthodox lowbridge layout were used in considerable numbers on both sides of the Mersey and remained in the company's fleet in diminishing numbers until the late sixties, though in their later years they were rarely seen on Merseyside. Lighter trafficked routes received some Leyland-Beadle chassisless saloons using running units taken from pre-war diesel engined Cubs. The 8ft wide KSW double-deckers, known as 'tanks' by Liverpool crews, were used in both high and lowbridge form from 1951-52 and in the following year the company took delivery of one of the six pre-production Bristol Lodekkas, a model which combined low height with pairs of seats and centre gangways on both decks. The rugged, durable and economical Lodekka, with its 13ft 4in overall height and roomy upper deck layout, became the standard workhorse from 1954. Few single-deckers were needed by Crosville but the 30ft long underfloor engined vehicle had arrived and the Bristol LS chassis was used mainly for coaches and dual-purpose vehicles. The latter were useful at Merseyside depots where they could be used on service from Monday to Friday and on the North Wales express routes at weekends.

In 1958 the fleet numbering system was changed, elements of systems used by other ex-Tilling companies being adopted. Each bus had a three letter prefix and a number. There were two numerical series, one for single-deckers and one for double-deckers; the first prefix letter indicated the type of vehicle, the second the chassis and the third the engine. Thus all double-deckers were D (until 1980 when H was introduced for full height), but single-deckers were sub-divided into S (ordinary bus), E (express bus or dual purpose) and C (coach). Thus, when a vehicle batch included buses with different engines, the prefixes would vary e.g. DLB – a Lodekka with a Bristol engine or DLG with a Gardner engine. If a single-deck vehicle was down-graded, the first letter would change but the remainder would remain thus CMG to EMG. The following year, the route number system was also revised, using a prefix letter for each area and a number; in some cases this created a need for changes to the destination equipment.

The 1958-59 vehicles were fitted with two-leaf hand-operated doors and thereafter rear platform doors became universal on all new deliveries. The last LD6s, which entered service in 1960, were the first with hopper windows and the Cave-Brown-Cave heating system, with which Crosville had been experimenting since 1957.

In 1960, a new series of Lodekkas, the FS, replaced the LD followed the next year by the 30ft long forward entrance FLF which had a noticeably more upright front, seats for 70 passengers and four-part power operated doors. The company took delivery of both types until 1966. Variety was provided by Lodekka coaches for the North Wales coast services. Periodically, as a new batch arrived, the older ones were downgraded to express buses and Liverpool depot had examples of both LD and FLF models in this category. A fleet of new FLFs with semi-automatic transmission replaced some of the older Lodekkas in Liverpool in 1968 and these were the last new front-engined buses to enter Crosville service.

Single-deck Policy

In 1968, Crosville's vehicle policy was changed to single-deck only though there was little demand for such vehicles in Liverpool. Bristol MWs and, from 1966-67, REs seating up to 53, were already in the fleet and the REs increased year by year. In 1971-72 the company purchased 100 Gardner-engined Seddon RU single-deck buses with bodies by the manufacturer of which half were 45-seat dual door (SPG class) and half were 47-seat dual purpose (EPG class). Both types were used for early one-man operation conversions with fare boxes, no tickets being issued, the SPGs in Wirral and the EPGs on both sides of the river. There was considerable fare evasion and the fare-boxes were replaced by Setright machines at the request of the PTE. The Seddons did not prove entirely satisfactory for the company's requirements, many being withdrawn in 1980-81.

During 1972, three Bristol SC4LK forward-engined, full fronted 35-seaters (SSG class), purchased in 1957 for lightly trafficked routes, ran in Liverpool with full crews. These had Gardner 4LK engines but were quite unsuitable for Liverpool traffic, but the management decided that all depots must lend double-deckers to Rhyl for the summer traffic. The SSGs were used indiscriminately on double-deck duties in Liverpool but the exercise was not repeated in subsequent years. On Route H5, Warrington depot occasionally supplied one of the vehicles transferred from the old Stockport-based North Western Road Car Co. Ltd when that company was broken up in 1972. Thus a Park Royal bodied AEC Renown or an Alexander bodied Daimler Fleetline would occasionally appear in the city.

Crosville was one of the first users of the Leyland

Leyland Titan TD7 M106 (BFN937) was one of ten buses with lowbridge Park Royal bodies diverted from East Kent to Crosville early in the war. In this post-war view at Heswall, note the single line front destination indicator which replaced the much larger East Kent style aperture originally fitted, supplemented by the Widd plate showing 'HESWALL PENSBY WOODSIDE' in the rear nearside window. Certain of these were rebodied by the company at Crane Wharf and included some parts from scrapped ex-Sheffield Craven bodies as shown in the lower view of M101. This type was withdrawn in 1958.

Sixteen Park Royal-bodied Leyland TD7s (M111-126), ordered by Southdown Motor Services Ltd., were diverted to Crosville in 1940. Although registered in Brighton, they came direct from Park Royal and the Crosville destination layout was incorporated from new. These were the first highbridge double deck buses to be purchased since the Leviathans of 1925. Ten of them were fitted with new bodies similar to M101 above in 1952-53.

The second-hand purchases during the wartime and post-war period produced some strange mixtures of chassis and bodies. Leyland buses were preferred but L131 was an AEC Regent, new in 1931 to Exeter Corporation and sold by them to Bristol Tramways & Carriage Co. in 1945. It was on hire to Crosville from December 1948 and purchased in October 1949. The body shown here came from UF 5644, a 1929 TD1 new to Southdown but sold to Western SMT Co. in 1938. This bus had been bought by Crosville in 1946 and numbered M248. It was rebodied by Eastern Coach Works in August 1949 and the old body used to replace the former highbridge body on L131. Note the higher 'piano front', a relic of the original Southdown destination layout. The bus is seen at West Kirby Wirral Station in July 1951; it was withdrawn in 1952.

Plymouth Corporation was the original owner of M235, a 1932 Leyland TD2 with Mumford lowbridge which entered the Crosville fleet as L79 in 1945, being fitted with a Leyland 8.6 litre diesel engine in January 1946 when the body was rebuilt by Eastern Coach Works. The Tilling indicator has a distinct 'added-on' appearance on account of the steep front rake. The bus is standing in Delamere Street, Chester, the former terminus of the Meols services.

It was a sign of the times that the Banks Road local service, worked by a Leyland Cub pre-war, now needed a double-decker as seen in this view of M245, a Leyland TD2 new to Western SMT Co. in 1932 and sold to Crosville in 1946. It received this new Eastern Coach Works body, of the type being fitted to new Bristol vehicles and a Covrad radiator in January 1949. The chassis was scrapped in 1956 but the body was transferred to Bristol K6A MB256.

This highbridge bus, seen in Market Square, Chester was No. L114 (WF 4735), a Brush-bodied Leyland TD2, new in 1932 to Binnington's Motors Ltd., Willerby and later East Yorkshire Motor Services. A new body with the distinctively-curved 'Beverley Bar' roof was fitted in 1936. This bus was purchased by Crosville in 1948 being based at Rock Ferry until scrapped in 1952.

National integrally-built single-deck bus, 24 of the first 11.3m production models joining the fleet in 1972; these had 44-seat dual-door bodies. Substantial numbers joined the fleet from 1974 onwards, the next examples having 48 dual-purpose seats, only one less than the front-entrance bus version. These were often to be seen on the Chester-Runcorn-Liverpool services. Crosville took both 10.3m and 11.3m versions of the National but until 1981 when the first National 2s were acquired, they were careful to avoid any more dual-door models having found that one-man operation did not need the body-weakening complication of two doors. Many of the earlier Nationals had their Leyland engines replaced by Gardner 6LXBs, many taken from the scrapped Seddons, from 1983 onwards, giving them a new lease of life.

One-man Double-deckers

While the Lodekka was a trouble free vehicle, it was unsuitable for one-man operation and, after the signing of the PTE/NBC agreement in January 1972, the PTE showed increasing signs of impatience at Crosville's lack of progress in the one-man double-deck field. Finally, in the second half of 1974, in response to PTE pressure, nine rear-engined Bristol VRs were temporarily diverted from Potteries Motor Traction Co. (PMT) to Crosville. They arrived new in Crosville livery but with PMT as the legal owner and were given the temporary fleet numbers DVG610-8. In March 1975 the first Crosville VRs arrived, being shared by Liverpool, Warrington and Heswall depots and, following a fire at PMT's Newcastle depot, their nine buses were hastily recalled being partially replaced by Ribble 1301 and 1369 on hire. Typically, Crosville produced a new class designation and renumbered them DAL701 and 769.

The Bristol VRT was the NBC's answer to the Leyland Atlantean and Daimler Fleetline. It had a 74-seat Eastern Coach Works body and rear mounted transverse engine. Because of its now rejected single-deck policy, Crosville missed some of the model's teething problems but it proved unequal to the arduous conditions on Merseyside where the fleet was worked very hard indeed. As the one-man conversions progressed, the reliable Lodekkas were replaced by the new model; seven Lodekkas remained to work H1 and 76 until March 1981. Because of a shortage of Gardner engines, following a strike at the Patricroft factory, many VRs had Leyland 500 series engines and these were concentrated in NBC's Western Region, at that time including Crosville and Ribble. Whilst this power unit gave better acceleration and a higher top speed, useful attributes on one-man city service, reliability and economy suffered. Brake wear was so heavy that some buses required a reline every 8-11 days and a special night shift was set up at Edge Lane to do just that.

In 1980, six second-hand VRs and 30 Fleetlines were purchased of which a few operated in Liverpool. One of the VRs with East Lancs. bodies, bought from South Yorkshire PTE and three of the Fleetlines from Southdown, were used

The 8ft wide Bristol KSW6B came in both lowbridge and highbridge form, the squat appearance of lowbridge MW493, new in 1953, seen standing in the Square, Neston en route from Woodside to Parkgate in February 1957 contrasting with the much more elegant lines of the full height DKB434 (formerly MW434) seen loading at Woodside for Chester (direct). Both buses have lost their upper cream bands, no doubt at the first repaint.

Three Crosville coaches caught by the camera at the Pier Head parking ground on 5th April 1952. On the left KW169 was a typical Bristol L6B with rear entrance Eastern Coach Works body, the standard Tilling Group single-deck bus of the post-war period. New in 1950, the reversed livery indicates that is a dual-purpose, a bus body with coach seating. In the centre is Bedford OB SL39, a 1949 Duple-bodied 29-seater bought for private hire and excursion work and rarely, if ever, used on service. Note the curved roof lights. The right-hand vehicle is KW258, a 1951 Bristol LWL6B with 35 seats. They were nick-named 'Queen Marys' and it will be noted that green has been eliminated from the livery, chrome strips being the only relief to the cream livery.

Seen on the Birkenhead-Parkgate service against a background of the 1860s Woodside ferry terminal building, 1966 Bristol RELL6G ERG595 was equipped for one man operation from new. Delivered in cream livery with a green waistband, it was repainted as shown with the interim lower case fleet title which preceded NBC corporate styles.

on the Dublin boat contract. After the move to Love Lane depot, one would frequently be used to ferry drivers to and from Mann Island terminus. Two ex-Southdown Fleetlines with 71-seat Northern Counties bodies (HDG910/4), dating from 1970, were used as Garden Festival buses in 1984, with ex-South Yorkshire VR HVG933 as stand-by. Immediately prior to deregulation, the fleet at Love Lane comprised 65 vehicles of which 50 were VRs.

A great many second-hand vehicles from other NBC companies were taken into the Crosville fleet in the eighties, some as spares but others as cheap replacements for older vehicles. Ten Merseyside PTE Daimler Fleetlines went on long loan at Heswall depot in 1983 being repainted in Crosville colours but retaining PTE legal owner names.

The double-deck bus of the eighties was undoubtedly the Leyland Olympian and the first of 30 Crosville examples went into service at West Kirby and Heswall in 1982-83. They had Eastern Coach Works bodies and were given the intriguing classification DOG. The next five (DOG131-5) were the first Olympians for the NBC to be built at the Leyland Workington factory. Even 49-seat Nationals were replaced by 77-seat Olympians at West Kirby in 1983.

Just prior to deregulation, substantial orders were placed for a large fleet of minibuses. Six Mercedes Benz L608D, converted from vans to 20-seat buses by Reeve Burgess, stayed only a short time before being temporarily exchanged with Alder Valley North for the same number of Freight Rover Sherpas with 16-seat Dormobile bodies. There were soon 88 of these in the fleet of which 16 were immediately hired to Merseybus whose minibus order had not been fulfilled.

The Coach Fleet

The pioneer summer season daily express services were largely run with charabancs or canvas-roofed coaches. When the London services started in 1929 something better was needed and four Leyland Tiger TS2 vehicles, (175-8) with standard angular Leyland bus bodies were fitted with coach seats and roof-mounted luggage racks. Two were based at Liverpool and two at West Kirby. The following year they were replaced by six similar vehicles Nos.369-74, with hinged doors opening outwards, the earlier models being relegated to the Liverpool-Caernarfon service. Many coaches bore headboards describing the route and were thus dedicated to a particular service; later models had illuminated panels or place names inscribed on glass louvres. A distinctive grey and green livery was adopted for the coach fleet and small batches of new Tigers were added to the fleet each year, the London service always enjoying a superior standard. In the mid-'thirties, Harrington bodies were favoured. The company always maintained a high standard of passenger comfort and even in post-war days refused to sacrifice comfort for higher capacity.

The acquisitions of the mid-'thirties saw some non-standard coaches added to the fleet, the AEC Regals of Maxways, Wirral Motor Transport and Pearsons remaining on coach duties. There was also a high-floor AEC 'Q' coach taken over from Pearsons which remained with Crosville until 1946. Many of the acquired vehicles were given new dual-purpose Eastern Coach Works bodies in 1939 and remained in service until 1951-53.

The last pre-war style coaches were actually delivered

Seen on the forecourt of Chester's Liverpool Road depot, is Leyland-Beadle PC21. In 1950 Crosville arranged with bodybuilder Beadle to produce 20 integral vehicles, utilising running units and radiators from the diesel-engined Leyland Cubs (P class), new in 1935-37. Numbers PC17 and 21 were fitted with Leyland O.350 engines in 1952, necessitating the fitting of a protruding cowl as shown. The project was not a success, these two buses being withdrawn in 1954; that shown was acquired by British Railways at Shrewsbury. The others, re-engined by Perkins, lasted until 1959.

A contrast in forward-entrance Bristol Lodekka styling. DFG75 (upper) was a short FSF6G, entering service in June 1962 and was one of the last buses to have the upper cream band. It is seen at Woodside on the Chester direct service. The more upright front of DFB202, an FLF6G gives it a more severe appearance which is alleviated by the restyled radiator grille and the rear wheel discs. It is seen turning from Duke Street into Beckwith Street, the Birkenhead Park Station terminus, when new.

in 1940; they were Tiger TS8s KA166-8 and K116 (petrol-engined, so late in the day) all carrying a style of 33-seat Burlingham body associated with the immediate post-war years.

For the first four post-war years, Crosville had to manage with the pre-war coach fleet and consequently ordinary service buses or the few dual-purpose vehicles had to be used for duplication on the shorter express services. Nine Bedford/Duple OBs, delivered in 1949 and a further 18 the following year, were purchased for excursion work, being unsuitable for express services. The year 1950 saw the arrival of ten 31-seat dual-purpose Bristol L6Bs and 35 Leyland PS1s, diverted from Midland General, which were externally flashy but originally had bus seats. The first new style coaches were 15 Bristol 35-seat full-fronted LL6Bs, 8ft wide and described by Crosland-Taylor as the most comfortable coaches ever to come into the Crosville fleet; they were nicknamed 'Queen Marys' and were joined by 28 similar 7ft 6in wide vehicles. Many were employed on the London services, almost overwhelmed by the demand for seats to see the Festival of Britain exhibition in 1951. The following year the first underfloor engined Bristol LS6Gs arrived, with comfortable seating for 39 on a chassis often used for 41-seats by other operators. The total full size coach intake in 1951-53 was 69 vehicles after which there was a lull for five years except for the first batch of double-deck Lodekka coaches in 1954. There were several batches of dual-purpose vehicles to provide weekend augmentation with a reasonable standard of comfort.

From 1958, the preferred coach chassis was the Bristol MW with a similar seating configuration to its predecessor and batches of these were still being taken into stock after the 1964 appearance of the 47-seat 36ft long RELH6G. Two further batches of double-deck coaches, this time on the forward-entrance FLF chassis and with 55 seats, were commissioned in 1962 and 1964. The first of these, (DFB109-13), went into service on the Liverpool-Caernarfon route on 1st December 1962. Illuminated offside advertisement panels were adapted to carry the slogan 'MERSEYSIDE North Wales DAILY. The earlier vehicles were downgraded to dual-purpose standard and painted green; they were unpopular with staff because of their straight staircases and absence of upstairs mirrors. Small batches of Bedfords were acquired for excursion and private hire work.

In the seventies, the company turned once again to Leyland for its coaches, the well-tried Leopard with Duple bodywork taking over many of the coach duties under the National banner. More Leopards with Willowbrook bodywork went into service in 1981-82.

The first of the new generation of Leyland Tigers appeared in 1983, both Plaxton Paramount and Duple Laser bodies being specified, while 1984 saw the arrival of two Royal Tigers with Roe Doyen bodies, one of which had a Cummins engine. The pinnacle of coach sophistication was reached in 1985 when five Bova Futura coaches were delivered with coachwork to National Express Rapide specification but these were not seen on Merseyside.

There were several transfers of coaches between Crosville and its neighbour, Ribble; five Leopards were in the company's fleet twice with an interregnum with Ribble. Finally there were the six double-deck three-axle Metroliners used on the Trans-Pennine services whose stay with Crosville was so short.

DAF-Optare 808 in the PMT fleet worked briefly from Chester depot but returned to Burslem. It is seen entering Ellesmere Port bus station in 23rd March 1991 on route 3 between Chester and Rivacre.

LIVERIES

From early days, Crosville buses were finished in grey and, after the period when buses carried names, a large fleet name CROSVILLE with an equally oversize fleet number below, appeared each side, lined out in dark red. The fleet name was originally proceeded by 'No.' but this was omitted from some buses later in the 'twenties.

In 1926 it was decided to experiment with a bright red livery and No. 210, the last of the first batch of 10 PLSC1 Lions was painted in this colour with a simple gilt lining stripe. No more were done for about six months but several were painted in 1927 and some earlier vehicles including Leviathans, which had cream upper works were repainted thus. The company, however, still traded as Crosville 'Grey' Motor Services. The first Titan double-decker, 325, was delivered in the red livery.

Purchase of the company by the LMS Railway in 1929 brought in its train the maroon livery similar, but not identical to the railway's passenger carriage colours. Titan TD1 367 was the first, ready for display at the Commercial Motor Show and Lion LT1 346 and possibly PLSC3 No. 31 were the only buses to have the original oval logo with LMS at the top and the fleet number at the bottom of the oval. The full LMS crest was carried on the rear. There was an all-over maroon version with the old style of fleet title and number. After BAT investment in 1930, the oval was retained but the fleet number replaced 'LMS' at the top of the oval and 'Motor Services' was fitted in below 'Crosville'. The LMS crest was replaced by a Crosville garter.

Except on double-deckers, the maroon livery with the oval was unrelieved except for thin gilt lining on the waistline but from 1936 there was a reversion to the large underlined 'Crosville' in gilt letters with fleet numbers to match, carried just below a cream waistband. The Crosville became smaller and by 1939 serifed letters were used.

A grey and green coach livery was devised in the early thirties, the application varying with the body style. 'Crosville' was either in a garter or arched on a black background and in 1939 there were new versions with letters ascending in size. The overall effect was more pleasing than the post-war all cream paint scheme, eventually relieved by black window surrounds.

When the Tilling green livery was first applied in 1945, utility Bristol Ks M171-4 being the first new vehicles treated, the styling was similar to the maroon. The new post-war Bristols had more cream relief, the double-deckers having cream upper deck window surrounds, a feature which was soon phased out. These layouts were, of course, standard Tilling features over which the company had no control. Older double-deckers lost their cream bands one by one, leaving just one at cantrail level to relieve the monotony.

In the NBC period, Group directives to eliminate all cream relief on single-deckers were often ignored, giving Crosville buses a slightly improved version of a very uninspiring 'leaf green' livery.

A great many coaches carried the white National Express colours and some were also finished in the somewhat similar National Holidays livery. Other coaches acquired the Town Lynx of which there were two versions. The main components were white, light green and dark green with red fleet titles and the new leaping lynx motif. This was the first departure from the dull stereotypes of the Wood era. Just prior to deregulation, Crosville buses assumed a new livery. The drab leaf green NBC colours were giving way to Brunswick green with, at first orange roofs and bands but this was soon changed to cream. A new Crosville logo embodying the leaping lynx finished off the new colour scheme.

The PMT era brought confusion with all kinds of paint and logo combinations being seen as a result of the transfer of vehicles from the Stoke-on-Trent fleet. In the summer of 1991, painting contractors were engaged on repainting Crosville Olympians in PMT red and yellow livery with large 'DOG' fleet numbers initially with no fleet title.

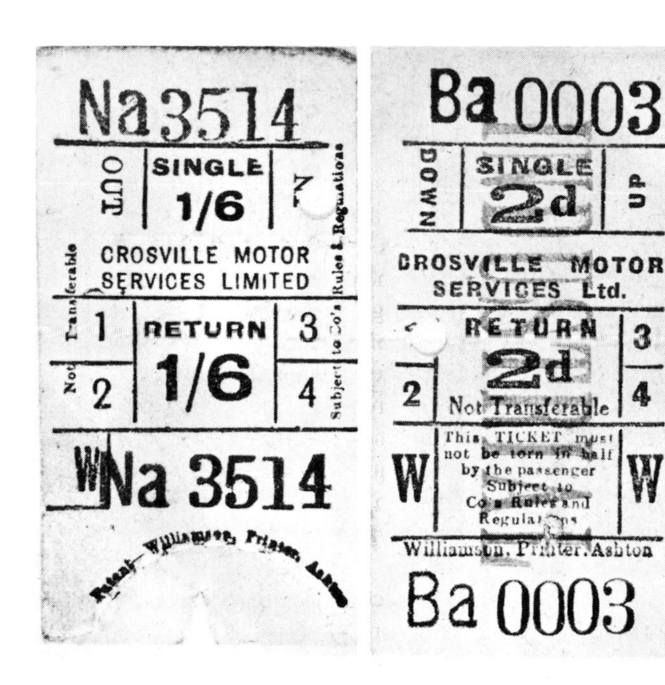

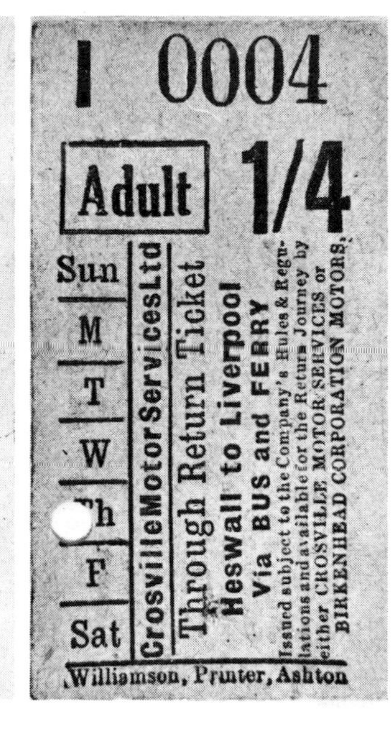

Four examples of Crosville Bell Punch tickets from the 'thirties when conductors on the longer routes had to carry two racks. Crosville favoured a combined single and return format; if issued as a return it was punched in the lower section and, on the return journey, the top was torn off by the conductor who issued a No Value Exchange ticket punched in the price. The number of top sections handed in had to agree with the number of exchanges issued. Each ticket value had a distinctive colour in a series of 14 colours which repeated in the same order into the higher values. The colour code included $1^{1}/_{2}$d and $2^{1}/_{2}$d but not the higher $^{1}/_{2}$d values which were abnormal and had special colours sometimes including stripes. The 1/6d is of a type in use in the early 'thirties, nailed in packs, the ticket being torn away from the perforated half moon on issue. This series was succeeded by the more sophisticated type represented by the 2d but many of the higher values rarely used remained of the old type. The 'Industrial' overprint was for use as a cheap return in Hoylake where very generous conditions applied up to 9.0am (instead of the more usual 8.0am) and also between 12 noon and 2.0pm. The 2d ticket was valid for a return journey between West Kirby and Hoylake or Hoylake and Meols at single fare. A similar series overprinted 'L C T' was used for journeys within the City of Liverpool.

The 1/4d Bus and Ferry return was one of a series ranging from 10d to 1/4d (with appropriate half fare child tickets) available on sections common with or adjacent to Birkenhead Corporation services. Although specifically printed for use between Heswall and Liverpool, a 1/4d fare was introduced from West Kirby via Irby Mill Hill in 1939 but little used and it is not known if a special ticket was issued for that fare. These tickets were eventually replaced by Setright insert tickets.

The Transfer Ticket was, in fact, nothing of the kind, being one of two types supplied by Crosville to Birkenhead Corporation who wanted payment for carrying Crosville season ticket holders. The Corporation would receive 5d for each of these tickets issued and $3^{1}/_{4}$d for similar tickets valid to Thingwall. There was no reciprocal arrangement as the Corporation issued contracts only from Thurstaston and Irby which were not served by Crosville buses from Woodside.

Summer Issue. 1934 P B 41.

MERSEYSIDE
TO
LLANDUDNO

COMBINED ROAD AND STEAMER SERVICES

BY ARRANGEMENT BETWEEN
CROSVILLE MOTOR SERVICES LTD.;
THE LIVERPOOL & NORTH WALES STEAMSHIP CO. LTD
C.C. 1/320. C.C. 1/332. C.C. 1/337.

Commencing SATURDAY, MAY 19th, 1934
and continuing until the termination of the Steamer Services on Monday, September 24th, 1934.
WEEKDAYS AND SUNDAYS (Bank Holidays excepted).
OUT BY STEAMER AND RETURN BY COACH (OR VICE VERSA).

NORTH WALES STEAMER.

LIVERPOOL (Princes Stage) dep. 10 45 a.m.	LLANDUDNO (Pier)	dep. 5 15 p.m.
LLANDUDNO (Pier) - - - arr. 1 5 p.m.	LIVERPOOL (Princes Stage)	arr. 7 30 p.m.

COACHES DEPART AND ARRIVE AS FOLLOWS:—

		a.m.	a.m.	
LIVERPOOL (Pier Head, Mann Island) -	dep.	—	—	
BIRKENHEAD (Woodside) - - -	,,	—	10 30	
WALLASEY (Seacombe Ferry) - -	,,	9 25	—	
LLANDUDNO (Coach Station, Oxford Rd.)	arr.	1 20 p.m.	1 0 p.m.	
		p.m.	p.m.	Passengers returning to Liverpool must pay their own Ferry Fee of 2d. from Birkenhead.
LLANDUDNO (Coach Station, Oxford Rd.)	dep.	6 0	6 30	
BIRKENHEAD (Woodside) - - -	arr.	8 35	—	
WALLASEY (Seacombe Ferry) - -	,,	—	10 25	
LIVERPOOL (Mann Island) - -	,,	—	—	

RETURN FARE from LIVERPOOL, BIRKENHEAD or WALLASEY

BY STEAMER **8/-** OR COACH

AVAILABLE DAY OF ISSUE ONLY.

S.S. St. TUDNO.

For Conditions of Booking and Offices see overleaf.

557. 5M. 6/34. G.R.G. Ltd.

A popular excursion during the 'thirties was a trip to Llandudno, one way by coach and the other by steamer at a fare of 8/- (40p).

Competitors

Hardings' is the oldest transport business in the north to have remained in the same family, having been founded in 1891 and is still going strong 101 years later. Alfred Harding's purchase of Johnston Brothers' Heswall service in 1924 caused Crosville some anxiety and this service was quickly bought out. This McCurd 4-ton charabanc seems to have an all-female load.

Macdonald and Co.'s 'Maxways' service competed strongly with Crosville between Birkenhead and Caernarfon and there were ten AEC Regal coaches in the fleet at the time the business was sold in December 1934. They carried names of Welsh castles and this one, new in 1932, became Crosville's T11, running until 1952 after rebodying.

Pearson's 'Happy Days' tried unsuccessfully to establish a foothold on the North Wales coast route and, at the time of its acquisition jointly by Crosville and Ribble in 1935, it was the last remaining independent operator on the Liverpool-London service. The livery was yellow with a red roof. The vehicle pictured before registration was probably KF 3756, a 1930 Leyland Tiger TS1 with Burlingham body which became Crosville K93. With a new Eastern Coach Works body fitted in 1939, it continued in service until 1952.

1st SUMMER ISSUE  1st SUMMER ISSUE

1932

CO-ORDINATED EXPRESS COACH SERVICES

LIVERPOOL

BIRKENHEAD—NEW FERRY—ABERGELE—LLANDUDNO—
BANGOR—CAERNARVON, AND RHYL

With Crosville Connections to

ANGLESEY AND SOUTH CAERNARVONSHIRE

Commencing WEDNESDAY, MAY 4th, 1932, until further notice.

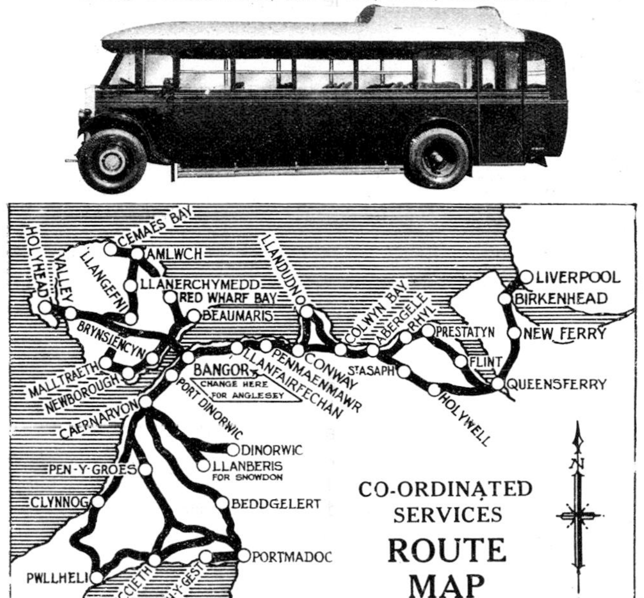

20,000—4.32. G.R.G. Ltd.

Under pressure from the Traffic Commissioners, the three North Wales express operators ran a co-ordinated service 1932-33 but Maxways opted out in 1934, their last year, thereby curtailing their service at Birkenhead. The introduction was postponed until 11th May.

"MAXWAYS"

CASTLE LINE

NORTH WALES COAST SERVICES.

For further particulars and Bookings, apply—

"MAXWAYS"

(Proprietors - MACDONALD & CO.)

Adjoining Woodside Hotel,

BIRKENHEAD.

Phones - Birkenhead 4000 (3 lines). Caernarvon 249.

Maxways' last time-table, their business being acquired by Crosville on 1st December 1934.

"MAXWAYS," 4, Chester St., BIRKENHEAD. Phone, Birkenhead 4000 (3 lines.).

OUTWARD JOURNEY.—	BIRKENHEAD to CAERNARVON.					Sats. only.	Fares from BIRKENHEAD	
	a.m.†	a.m.	p.m.	p.m.†	p.m.	p.m.	Single. s. d.	Return s. d.
BIRKENHEAD, "Maxways" Office	9 30	10 30	1 30	5 30	7 30	1 30		
Queensferry, Cross Roads	10 10	11 10	2 10	6 10	8 10	—	2 0	3 0
Connah's Quay (Hippodrome)	—	11 12	2 12	—	8 12	—	2 0	3 0
Flint (Poumphrey's Garage)	—	11 20	2 20	—	8 20	—	2 6	4 0
Bagillt (Cenotaph)	—	11 25	2 25	—	8 25	—	2 6	4 0
Greenfield (Packet House)	—	11 30	2 30	—	8 30	—	3 0	4 6
Mostyn (Mostyn Hotel)	—	11 35	2 35	—	8 35	E	3 0	4 6
Ffynnongroew (Farmers Arms)	—	11 37	2 37	—	8 37	X	3 6	5 0
Talacre(Tyn-y-Morfa)	—	11 43	2 43	—	8 43	P	3 6	5 0
Gronant (Cross Roads)	—	11 45	2 45	—	8 45	R	3 6	5 0
Northop (Wakeley's Garage)	10 20	—	—	6 20	—	E	2 6	4 0
Holywell (Victoria Hotel)	10 35	—	—	6 35	—	S	3 0	4 6
Rhuallt (Smithy Arms)	10 55	—	—	6 55	—	S	4 6	6 0
Prestatyn (Fire Station)	—	11 55	2 55	—	8 55	—	4 0	5 6
St. Asaph (Jones and Roberts)	11 0	—	—	7 0	—	—	4 6	6 0
Bodelwyddan (Robert's Cafe)	11 20	—	—	7 5	—	—	4 6	6 0
Rhyl (Midland Cafe, Promenade)	—	12X15	3X15	—	9X15	—	4 6	6 0
Rhuddlan (King's Head Hotel)	—	12 20	3 20	—	9 20	—	4 6	6 0
Abergele (H. C. Williams, P.O. Buildings)	11 30	12 35	3 35	7 30	9 35	—	4 6	6 6
Llandulas (Railway Hotel)	11 37	12 45	3 45	7 37	9 45	—	5 0	7 0
Old Colwyn (Red Booking Office)	11 45	12 50	3 50	7 45	9 50	—	5 0	7 0
Colwyn Bay (Red Booking Office, Penrhyn Road)	11 50	12 55	3 55	7 50	9 55	3 30	5 6	7 6
Llandudno (Red Garage, Mostyn Street)	12 0	1 5	4 5	8 0	10 5	—	6 0	8 0
Deganwy (Lancaster & Co. Stationers)	12 5	1 10	—	8 5	—	—	6 0	8 0
Llandudno Junction (Level Crossing)	12 10	1 15	—	8 10	—	3 40	6 0	8 0
Conway (H. Moody, Lancaster Square)	12 15	1 20	—	8 15	—	3 45	6 0	8 0
Penmaenmawr (Robert's Garage)	12 25	1 30	—	8 25	—	3 55	6 0	8 0
Llanfairfechan (Goodall's Cafe)	12 35	1 40	—	8 35	—	4 5	6 6	8 6
Aber (Falls Halt)	12 40	1 45	—	8 40	—	4 10	7 0	9 0
Bangor (Corporation Parking Ground)	1 0	2 0	—	9 0	—	4 30	7 0	9 0
Portdinorwic (Jones' Garage)	1 15	—	—	9 15	—	4 45	7 6	9 6
Caernarvon (Castle Square)	1 30	—	—	9 30	—	5 0	8 0	10 0

SUNDAYS ONE HOUR LATER AT ALL STAGES.

(Change at Caernarvon for Pwllheli, 12/6, and Nevin, 13/-). X Arrives 10 mins. earlier. † Denotes all year round service.

ACKNOWLEDGMENTS

Much of the material in this book has been gathered over many years and the author had the benefit of personal contributions by three eminent busmen who, unhappily, are no longer with us – C.R. Buckley, D.S. Deacon and H.H. Merchant – all of whom learnt much of their trade with Crosville on Merseyside in their formative years and moved on to high office elsewhere later in life.

Thanks are also due to J.N. Barlow, W. Barlow, J.E. Dunabin, P.L. Hardy, G. Parry, D. Randall, P.F. Rusk, K.W. Swallow, D.N. Thompson (Archivist, Wirral Borough Libraries), T.G. Turner and J. Webster for valuable assistance and to B.J. Rusk, J.P. Williams and R.L. Wilson for permission to reproduce photographs. Special thanks are due to D.J. Meredith, former Managing Director of the company, for reading the text and offering helpful suggestions.

The fleet history publications of the PSV Circle and Omnibus Society have been invaluable aids.

AUTHOR'S NOTE

It might be argued that a book entitled Crosville on Merseyside should contain details of local services in Runcorn and perhaps even Warrington. However, space considerations led to the decision to confine coverage to the 1974 Merseyside county plus Ellesmere Port and Neston.

OTHER READING ON CROSVILLE

Crosville – The Sowing and the Harvest, W.J. Crosland-Taylor TPC 1987

State Owned Without Tears, W.J. Crosland-Taylor TPC 1987

A History of Crosville Motor Services, R.C. Anderson David and Charles, 1981.

The Best of British Buses No. 5 – 75 Years of Crosville - John Carroll TPC 1981

Crosville in Wirral – T.B. Maund – featured in Buses Extra Nos. 43, Oct. 1986 & 65, June 1990. Ian Allan

Leyland Swift No. 320 carries Crosville lettering but retained PMT fleet number 320. Based at Chester, it is seen at West Kirby station on route 23 (formerly C23) to its home city.

This 29-seat Mercedes Benz 811D, seen on a local service in Ellesmere Port, is PMT No. 360 and has bodywork by the operator.